Microsoft Office Visio
Complete Self-Assessment Guide

The guidance in this Self-Assessment is based on Microsoft Office Visio best practices and standards in business process architecture, design and quality management. The guidance is also based on the professional judgment of the individual collaborators listed in the Acknowledgments.

Notice of rights

Trademarks

Table of Contents

About The Art of Service

The Art of Service, Business Process Architects since 2000, is dedicated to helping stakeholders achieve excellence.

Defining, designing, creating, and implementing a process to solve a stakeholders challenge or meet an objective is the most valuable role... In EVERY group, company, organization and department.

Unless you're talking a one-time, single-use project, there should be a process. Whether that process is managed and implemented by humans, AI, or a combination of the two, it needs to be designed by someone with a complex enough perspective to ask the right questions.

Someone capable of asking the right questions and step back and say, 'What are we really trying to accomplish here? And is there a different way to look at it?'

With The Art of Service's Standard Requirements Self-Assessments, we empower people who can do just that — whether their title is marketer, entrepreneur, manager, salesperson, consultant, Business Process Manager, executive assistant, IT Manager, CIO etc... —they are the people who rule the future. They are people who watch the process as it happens, and ask the right questions to make the process work better.

Contact us when you need any support with this Self-Assessment and any help with templates, blue-prints and examples of standard documents you might need:

http://theartofservice.com
service@theartofservice.com

Included Resources - how to access

Included with your purchase of the book is the Microsoft Office

Visio Self-Assessment Spreadsheet Dashboard which contains all questions and Self-Assessment areas and auto-generates insights, graphs, and project RACI planning - all with examples to get you started right away.

How? Simply send an email to
access@theartofservice.com
with this books' title in the subject to get the Microsoft Office Visio Self Assessment Tool right away.

You will receive the following contents with New and Updated specific criteria:

- The latest quick edition of the book in PDF

- The latest complete edition of the book in PDF, which criteria correspond to the criteria in...

- The Self-Assessment Excel Dashboard, and...

- Example pre-filled Self-Assessment Excel Dashboard to get familiar with results generation

- In-depth specific Checklists covering the topic

- Project management checklists and templates to assist with implementation

INCLUDES LIFETIME SELF ASSESSMENT UPDATES

Every self assessment comes with Lifetime Updates and Lifetime Free Updated Books. Lifetime Updates is an industry-first feature which allows you to receive verified self assessment updates, ensuring you always have the most accurate information at your fingertips.

Get it now- you will be glad you did - do it now, before you forget.

Send an email to **access@theartofservice.com** with this books' title in the subject to get the Microsoft Office Visio Self Assessment Tool right away.

Purpose of this Self-Assessment

This Self-Assessment has been developed to improve understanding of the requirements and elements of Microsoft Office Visio, based on best practices and standards in business process architecture, design and quality management.

It is designed to allow for a rapid Self-Assessment to determine how closely existing management practices and procedures correspond to the elements of the Self-Assessment.

The criteria of requirements and elements of Microsoft Office Visio have been rephrased in the format of a Self-Assessment questionnaire, with a seven-criterion scoring system, as explained in this document.

In this format, even with limited background knowledge of Microsoft Office Visio, a manager can quickly review existing operations to determine how they measure up to the standards. This in turn can serve as the starting point of a 'gap analysis' to identify management tools or system elements that might usefully be implemented in the organization to help improve overall performance.

How to use the Self-Assessment

On the following pages are a series of questions to identify to what extent your Microsoft Office Visio initiative is complete in comparison to the requirements set in standards.

To facilitate answering the questions, there is a space in front of each question to enter a score on a scale of '1' to '5'.

1 Strongly Disagree

2 Disagree

3 Neutral

4 Agree

5 Strongly Agree

Read the question and rate it with the following in front of mind:

'In my belief,
the answer to this question is clearly defined'.

There are two ways in which you can choose to interpret this statement;
1. how aware are you that the answer to the question is clearly defined
2. for more in-depth analysis you can choose to gather evidence and confirm the answer to the question. This obviously will take more time, most Self-Assessment users opt for the first way to interpret the question and dig deeper later on based on the outcome of the overall Self-Assessment.

A score of '1' would mean that the answer is not clear at all, where a '5' would mean the answer is crystal clear and defined. Leave emtpy when the question is not applicable or you don't want to answer it, you can skip it without affecting your score. Write your score in the space provided.

After you have responded to all the appropriate statements in each section, compute your average score for that section, using the formula provided, and round to the nearest tenth. Then transfer to the corresponding spoke in the Microsoft Office Visio Scorecard on the second next page of the Self-Assessment.

Your completed Microsoft Office Visio Scorecard will give you a clear presentation of which Microsoft Office Visio areas need attention.

Microsoft Office Visio Scorecard Example

Example of how the finalized Scorecard can look like:

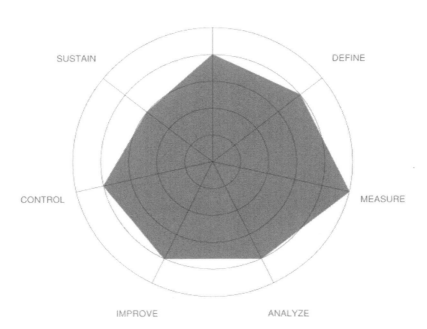

Microsoft Office Visio Scorecard

Your Scores:

BEGINNING OF THE SELF-ASSESSMENT:

CRITERION #1: RECOGNIZE

INTENT: Be aware of the need for change. Recognize that there is an unfavorable variation, problem or symptom.

In my belief, the answer to this question is clearly defined:

5 Strongly Agree

4 Agree

3 Neutral

2 Disagree

1 Strongly Disagree

1. How much background information is needed?
<--- Score

2. What is the problem or issue?
<--- Score

3. Do you need an appendix for people who want more detail?
<--- Score

4. Is the ability to capture the transaction status codes needed to ensure workflow system integrity provided by the proposed system?

<--- Score

5. Would you need to reword or carefully word any part of your letter?

<--- Score

6. Are there any specific expectations or concerns about the Microsoft Office Visio team, Microsoft Office Visio itself?

<--- Score

7. Is this issue important to him/her?

<--- Score

8. Does Microsoft Office Visio create potential expectations in other areas that need to be recognized and considered?

<--- Score

9. What should be considered when identifying available resources, constraints, and deadlines?

<--- Score

10. As a sponsor, customer or management, how important is it to meet goals, objectives?

<--- Score

11. Does the proposed system enable modeling multiple escalation workflows based on problem type?

<--- Score

12. What activities does the governance board need to consider?
<--- Score

13. What dont they need to know?
<--- Score

14. How do you identify the sequence of the sub shapes in a group shape?
<--- Score

15. What microsoft office licenses do you need?
<--- Score

16. Looking at each person individually – does every one have the qualities which are needed to work in this group?
<--- Score

17. What training and capacity building actions are needed to implement proposed reforms?
<--- Score

18. What else needs to be measured?
<--- Score

19. What kinds of artistic skills do you need to use Visio?
<--- Score

20. Have you identified your Microsoft Office Visio key performance indicators?
<--- Score

21. Your organization has a unique story, and like any great tale, it needs people to make it come

alive. How do you get your employees excited about your vision?
<--- Score

22. What problems are you facing and how do you consider Microsoft Office Visio will circumvent those obstacles?
<--- Score

23. How much are sponsors, customers, partners, stakeholders involved in Microsoft Office Visio? In other words, what are the risks, if Microsoft Office Visio does not deliver successfully?
<--- Score

24. Why do you need Visio?
<--- Score

25. What situation(s) led to this Microsoft Office Visio Self Assessment?
<--- Score

26. How are you going to measure success?
<--- Score

27. Who else hopes to benefit from it?
<--- Score

28. Do you need to do any more research?
<--- Score

29. Are you dealing with any of the same issues today as yesterday? What can you do about this?
<--- Score

30. How do you assess your Microsoft Office Visio

workforce capability and capacity needs, including skills, competencies, and staffing levels?
<--- Score

31. When a Microsoft Office Visio manager recognizes a problem, what options are available?
<--- Score

32. Will Microsoft Office Visio deliverables need to be tested and, if so, by whom?
<--- Score

33. What, if any, level of training is needed in the use of the product and its features?
<--- Score

34. What are the stakeholder objectives to be achieved with Microsoft Office Visio?
<--- Score

35. Are there any revenue recognition issues?
<--- Score

36. How to customize workflow to meet operational needs without creating maintenance issues?
<--- Score

37. What are the expected benefits of Microsoft Office Visio to the stakeholder?
<--- Score

38. Who defines the rules in relation to any given issue?
<--- Score

39. What would happen if Microsoft Office Visio weren't done?
<--- Score

40. What prevents you from making the changes you know will make you a more effective Microsoft Office Visio leader?
<--- Score

41. Do you need to avoid or amend any Microsoft Office Visio activities?
<--- Score

42. What does your reader need or want?
<--- Score

43. What problems do you see in your writing?
<--- Score

44. Consider your own Microsoft Office Visio project, what types of organizational problems do you think might be causing or affecting your problem, based on the work done so far?
<--- Score

45. Are there recognized Microsoft Office Visio problems?
<--- Score

46. How do you take a forward-looking perspective in identifying Microsoft Office Visio research related to market response and models?
<--- Score

47. How are the Microsoft Office Visio's objectives aligned to the group's overall stakeholder strategy?

<--- Score

48. Do you know what you need to know about Microsoft Office Visio?
<--- Score

49. Why did your business system fail to prevent the error?
<--- Score

50. Are your goals realistic? Do you need to redefine your problem? Perhaps the problem has changed or maybe you have reached your goal and need to set a new one?
<--- Score

51. What issues should you know about?
<--- Score

52. What does Microsoft Office Visio success mean to the stakeholders?
<--- Score

53. What do they need to know?
<--- Score

54. How do you identify your purpose?
<--- Score

55. Are controls defined to recognize and contain problems?
<--- Score

56. Do you need different information or graphics?
<--- Score

57. What is the problem or issue?

<--- Score

58. The goal of the workflow. What need is it addressing?

<--- Score

59. Does your organization need more Microsoft Office Visio education?

<--- Score

60. Do I provide enough context for the assertion or is more background information needed?

<--- Score

61. Which information does the Microsoft Office Visio business case need to include?

<--- Score

62. What does your reader know and need to know?

<--- Score

63. To what extent does each concerned units management team recognize Microsoft Office Visio as an effective investment?

<--- Score

64. Are problem definition and motivation clearly presented?

<--- Score

65. Who needs to know about Microsoft Office Visio?

<--- Score

66. What is the current climate relating to this

issue?
<--- Score

67. What information is needed for the execution of each step?
<--- Score

68. Is the need for organizational change recognized?
<--- Score

69. Do you have/need 24-hour access to key personnel?
<--- Score

70. What needs to be done?
<--- Score

71. What are your needs in relation to Microsoft Office Visio skills, labor, equipment, and markets?
<--- Score

72. What is the Microsoft Office Visio problem definition? What do you need to resolve?
<--- Score

73. Can management personnel recognize the monetary benefit of Microsoft Office Visio?
<--- Score

74. What does the reader need to do?
<--- Score

75. How can auditing be a preventative security measure?
<--- Score

76. Will it solve real problems?
<--- Score

77. What extra resources will you need?
<--- Score

78. What level of staff support will you need?
<--- Score

79. Programming is one thing. Writing programs that meet the needs of the business is another. How do the business people and the programmers communicate?
<--- Score

Add up total points for this section:
_ _ _ _ _ = Total points for this section

Divided by: _ _ _ _ _ _ (number of statements answered) = _ _ _ _ _ _
Average score for this section

Transfer your score to the Microsoft Office Visio Index at the beginning of the Self-Assessment.

CRITERION #2: DEFINE:

INTENT: Formulate the stakeholder problem. Define the problem, needs and objectives.

In my belief, the answer to this question is clearly defined:

5 Strongly Agree

4 Agree

3 Neutral

2 Disagree

1 Strongly Disagree

1. Is special Microsoft Office Visio user knowledge required?
<--- Score

2. What sort of a use case fits your project?
<--- Score

3. Is the Microsoft Office Visio scope complete and appropriately sized?

<--- Score

4. What is the context?
<--- Score

5. What are the boundaries of the scope? What is in bounds and what is not? What is the start point? What is the stop point?
<--- Score

6. Has a team charter been developed and communicated?
<--- Score

7. How was the 'as is' process map developed, reviewed, verified and validated?
<--- Score

8. What Microsoft Office Visio requirements should be gathered?
<--- Score

9. Who are the Microsoft Office Visio improvement team members, including Management Leads and Coaches?
<--- Score

10. Is the Microsoft Office Visio scope manageable?
<--- Score

11. What is the purpose of requirements traceability?
<--- Score

12. Is there a critical path to deliver Microsoft Office Visio results?

<--- Score

13. What would be the goal or target for a Microsoft Office Visio's improvement team?
<--- Score

14. Is the current 'as is' process being followed? If not, what are the discrepancies?
<--- Score

15. Is the team equipped with available and reliable resources?
<--- Score

16. How do you keep key subject matter experts in the loop?
<--- Score

17. What happens if Microsoft Office Visio's scope changes?
<--- Score

18. How would you define the culture at your organization, how susceptible is it to Microsoft Office Visio changes?
<--- Score

19. Is there a Microsoft Office Visio management charter, including stakeholder case, problem and goal statements, scope, milestones, roles and responsibilities, communication plan?
<--- Score

20. Does the team have regular meetings?
<--- Score

21. Has the improvement team collected the 'voice of the customer' (obtained feedback – qualitative and quantitative)?
<--- Score

22. Scope of sensitive information?
<--- Score

23. Is Microsoft Office Visio currently on schedule according to the plan?
<--- Score

24. Has your organization clearly defined its initial Vision?
<--- Score

25. Is there a completed, verified, and validated high-level 'as is' (not 'should be' or 'could be') stakeholder process map?
<--- Score

26. Are customer(s) identified and segmented according to their different needs and requirements?
<--- Score

27. Has the Microsoft Office Visio work been fairly and/or equitably divided and delegated among team members who are qualified and capable to perform the work? Has everyone contributed?
<--- Score

28. How do you catch Microsoft Office Visio definition inconsistencies?
<--- Score

29. What are the dynamics of the communication

plan?

<--- Score

30. What are the Roles and Responsibilities for each team member and its leadership? Where is this documented?

<--- Score

31. What Microsoft Office Visio services do you require?

<--- Score

32. Are there any constraints known that bear on the ability to perform Microsoft Office Visio work? How is the team addressing them?

<--- Score

33. What is out-of-scope initially?

<--- Score

34. How often are the team meetings?

<--- Score

35. Will team members perform Microsoft Office Visio work when assigned and in a timely fashion?

<--- Score

36. Are accountability and ownership for Microsoft Office Visio clearly defined?

<--- Score

37. How do you hand over Microsoft Office Visio context?

<--- Score

38. How do you gather Microsoft Office Visio

requirements?
<--- Score

39. What key stakeholder process output measure(s) does Microsoft Office Visio leverage and how?
<--- Score

40. Are different versions of process maps needed to account for the different types of inputs?
<--- Score

41. What critical content must be communicated – who, what, when, where, and how?
<--- Score

42. Do the problem and goal statements meet the SMART criteria (specific, measurable, attainable, relevant, and time-bound)?
<--- Score

43. What information should you gather?
<--- Score

44. Have all basic functions of Microsoft Office Visio been defined?
<--- Score

45. What are the rough order estimates on cost savings/opportunities that Microsoft Office Visio brings?
<--- Score

46. What is in scope?
<--- Score

47. Are stakeholder processes mapped?

<--- Score

48. What customer feedback methods were used to solicit their input?
<--- Score

49. Which are requirements workflow tasks done in the inception phase?
<--- Score

50. How will the Microsoft Office Visio team and the group measure complete success of Microsoft Office Visio?
<--- Score

51. When is the estimated completion date?
<--- Score

52. What defines best in class?
<--- Score

53. How does the Microsoft Office Visio manager ensure against scope creep?
<--- Score

54. Have specific policy objectives been defined?
<--- Score

55. Are there different segments of customers?
<--- Score

56. Will the system have any workflow requirements?
<--- Score

57. What baselines are required to be defined and

managed?
<--- Score

58. When is/was the Microsoft Office Visio start date?
<--- Score

59. Who is gathering Microsoft Office Visio information?
<--- Score

60. How are consistent Microsoft Office Visio definitions important?
<--- Score

61. What specifically is the problem? Where does it occur? When does it occur? What is its extent?
<--- Score

62. Is there regularly 100% attendance at the team meetings? If not, have appointed substitutes attended to preserve cross-functionality and full representation?
<--- Score

63. What is the approach to make sure that applications do comply with the requirements?
<--- Score

64. Has a high-level 'as is' process map been completed, verified and validated?
<--- Score

65. Are improvement team members fully trained on Microsoft Office Visio?
<--- Score

66. When are meeting minutes sent out? Who is on the distribution list?
<--- Score

67. How will the context affect reader response?
<--- Score

68. Is the improvement team aware of the different versions of a process: what they think it is vs. what it actually is vs. what it should be vs. what it could be?
<--- Score

69. What scope do you want your strategy to cover?
<--- Score

70. What scope to assess?
<--- Score

71. What constraints exist that might impact the team?
<--- Score

72. Does the current environment support the business and functional requirements?
<--- Score

73. What are the assumptions upon which the business case is based?
<--- Score

74. Does the scope remain the same?
<--- Score

75. Will team members regularly document their Microsoft Office Visio work?
<--- Score

76. Is data collected and displayed to better understand customer(s) critical needs and requirements.
<--- Score

77. Has your scope been defined?
<--- Score

78. Is the team adequately staffed with the desired cross-functionality? If not, what additional resources are available to the team?
<--- Score

79. What sort of initial information to gather?
<--- Score

80. Do you require a content publishing workflow?
<--- Score

81. What are the record-keeping requirements of Microsoft Office Visio activities?
<--- Score

82. What system do you use for gathering Microsoft Office Visio information?
<--- Score

83. How did the Microsoft Office Visio manager receive input to the development of a Microsoft Office Visio improvement plan and the estimated completion dates/times of each activity?
<--- Score

84. Is the scope of Microsoft Office Visio defined?
<--- Score

85. Are required metrics defined, what are they?
<--- Score

86. What are the Microsoft Office Visio use cases?
<--- Score

87. How will variation in the actual durations of each activity be dealt with to ensure that the expected Microsoft Office Visio results are met?
<--- Score

88. Is there any additional Microsoft Office Visio definition of success?
<--- Score

89. Did you include enough details and examples to support your assertion?
<--- Score

90. Have the customer needs been translated into specific, measurable requirements? How?
<--- Score

91. Is Microsoft Office Visio linked to key stakeholder goals and objectives?
<--- Score

92. How have you defined all Microsoft Office Visio requirements first?
<--- Score

93. Are customers identified and high impact areas defined?
<--- Score

94. Is the team sponsored by a champion or stakeholder leader?

<--- Score

95. Has/have the customer(s) been identified?

<--- Score

96. Workflow; is oversight approval required?

<--- Score

97. If substitutes have been appointed, have they been briefed on the Microsoft Office Visio goals and received regular communications as to the progress to date?

<--- Score

98. Has anyone else (internal or external to the group) attempted to solve this problem or a similar one before? If so, what knowledge can be leveraged from these previous efforts?

<--- Score

99. How is the team tracking and documenting its work?

<--- Score

100. Is there a completed SIPOC representation, describing the Suppliers, Inputs, Process, Outputs, and Customers?

<--- Score

101. What are the compelling stakeholder reasons for embarking on Microsoft Office Visio?

<--- Score

102. How can the value of Microsoft Office Visio be

defined?

<--- Score

103. Does workflow allow users to define conditions?

<--- Score

104. What is the definition of success?

<--- Score

105. Do you have a Microsoft Office Visio success story or case study ready to tell and share?

<--- Score

106. Is full participation by members in regularly held team meetings guaranteed?

<--- Score

107. Which are requirements workflow tasks done in the elaboration phase?

<--- Score

108. Has a project plan, Gantt chart, or similar been developed/completed?

<--- Score

109. What are the resources and forensic tools required to preserve the original media?

<--- Score

110. Has everyone on the team, including the team leaders, been properly trained?

<--- Score

111. What do you do if the formatting is lost while exporting requirements to microsoft word?

<--- Score

112. Has the direction changed at all during the course of Microsoft Office Visio? If so, when did it change and why?
<--- Score

113. Is the team formed and are team leaders (Coaches and Management Leads) assigned?
<--- Score

114. Who is gathering information?
<--- Score

115. Is a fully trained team formed, supported, and committed to work on the Microsoft Office Visio improvements?
<--- Score

116. Is Microsoft Office Visio required?
<--- Score

117. Are team charters developed?
<--- Score

Add up total points for this section:
_ _ _ _ _ = Total points for this section

Divided by: _ _ _ _ _ _ (number of statements answered) = _ _ _ _ _ _ Average score for this section

Transfer your score to the Microsoft Office Visio Index at the beginning of the Self-Assessment.

CRITERION #3: MEASURE:

INTENT: Gather the correct data.
Measure the current performance and
evolution of the situation.

In my belief, the answer to this
question is clearly defined:

5 Strongly Agree

4 Agree

3 Neutral

2 Disagree

1 Strongly Disagree

1. What is the role of analysis?
<--- Score

2. How much does it cost?
<--- Score

3. What relevant entities could be measured?
<--- Score

4. Is there an opportunity to verify requirements?
<--- Score

5. Is it possible to estimate the impact of unanticipated complexity such as wrong or failed assumptions, feedback, etcetera on proposed reforms?
<--- Score

6. Was a business case (cost/benefit) developed?
<--- Score

7. Does the Microsoft Office Visio task fit the client's priorities?
<--- Score

8. Did you tackle the cause or the symptom?
<--- Score

9. How frequently do you track Microsoft Office Visio measures?
<--- Score

10. Are you taking your company in the direction of better and revenue or cheaper and cost?
<--- Score

11. What are the key input variables? What are the key process variables? What are the key output variables?
<--- Score

12. Is Process Variation Displayed/Communicated?
<--- Score

13. Which stakeholder characteristics are analyzed?
<--- Score

14. Is there a written policy and/or process flowchart defining the responsibilities of processing, recording, approval and distribution of payroll and of personnel activities?
<--- Score

15. How do you aggregate measures across priorities?
<--- Score

16. What is the cost of rework?
<--- Score

17. How can big data analytics be integrated into the workflow?
<--- Score

18. Is a solid data collection plan established that includes measurement systems analysis?
<--- Score

19. Does your organization systematically track and analyze outcomes related for accountability and quality improvement?
<--- Score

20. What steps in competitive research and analysis are involved?
<--- Score

21. What can be used to verify compliance?
<--- Score

22. Does devsecops also impact the management of open source projects?
<--- Score

23. What is measured? Why?
<--- Score

24. Who is involved in verifying compliance?
<--- Score

25. Have the types of risks that may impact Microsoft Office Visio been identified and analyzed?
<--- Score

26. Are you able to realize any cost savings?
<--- Score

27. Verify business objectives. Are they appropriate, and well-articulated?
<--- Score

28. Has a cost benefit analysis been performed?
<--- Score

29. How does cost-to-serve analysis help?
<--- Score

30. What could cause delays in the schedule?
<--- Score

31. How will measures be used to manage and adapt?
<--- Score

32. When a disaster occurs, who gets priority?
<--- Score

33. What is the total fixed cost?
<--- Score

34. What are the operational costs after Microsoft Office Visio deployment?
<--- Score

35. At what cost?
<--- Score

36. How will you describe the technology, secret sauce, or magic behind your product or service. The less text and the more diagrams, schematics and flowcharts the better. What do you have that makes your better?
<--- Score

37. Where can you go to verify the info?
<--- Score

38. Who should receive measurement reports?
<--- Score

39. Do you effectively measure and reward individual and team performance?
<--- Score

40. What charts has the team used to display the components of variation in the process?
<--- Score

41. What are the agreed upon definitions of the high impact areas, defect(s), unit(s), and opportunities that will figure into the process capability metrics?
<--- Score

42. Have changes been properly/adequately analyzed for effect?
<--- Score

43. Browse through corporate Web sites to identify different indicators of corporate culture. If you dont know your audience, how can you analyze it?
<--- Score

44. How frequently do you verify your Microsoft Office Visio strategy?
<--- Score

45. Was a data collection plan established?
<--- Score

46. When are costs are incurred?
<--- Score

47. What is your cost benefit analysis?
<--- Score

48. Are the units of measure consistent?
<--- Score

49. Does the staff conduct periodic analysis comparing projected with actual performance (variance analysis)?
<--- Score

50. What particular quality tools did the team find helpful in establishing measurements?
<--- Score

51. How do you control the overall costs of your work processes?
<--- Score

52. What are the types and number of measures to

use?
<--- Score

53. Has a cost center been established?
<--- Score

54. Have you ever done a cost-benefit analysis?
<--- Score

55. Is there a Performance Baseline?
<--- Score

56. Are high impact defects defined and identified in the stakeholder process?
<--- Score

57. Are all the shapes in your diagram labeled?
<--- Score

58. What key measures identified indicate the performance of the stakeholder process?
<--- Score

59. How do your measurements capture actionable Microsoft Office Visio information for use in exceeding your customers expectations and securing your customers engagement?
<--- Score

60. Is key measure data collection planned and executed, process variation displayed and communicated and performance baselined?
<--- Score

61. What is the impact if the entire system had to be reloaded using disaster recovery backup

procedures?
<--- Score

62. For each proposed process alternative, did the team include a detailed workflow and a thorough description of impacts on other processes and the overall work environment?
<--- Score

63. What are the uncertainties surrounding estimates of impact?
<--- Score

64. Have all non-recommended alternatives been analyzed in sufficient detail?
<--- Score

65. If you do not know your audience, how can you analyze it?
<--- Score

66. How will you measure your Microsoft Office Visio effectiveness?
<--- Score

67. How will you measure success?
<--- Score

68. What Is BPAs Impact on Business Workflow?
<--- Score

69. How do you verify the Microsoft Office Visio requirements quality?
<--- Score

70. How is the value delivered by Microsoft Office

Visio being measured?
<--- Score

71. How do you verify performance?
<--- Score

72. How can big data analytics be integrated into the clinical workflow?
<--- Score

73. What makes a good analysis?
<--- Score

74. How do you verify if Microsoft Office Visio is built right?
<--- Score

75. How large is the gap between current performance and the customer-specified (goal) performance?
<--- Score

76. What are your key Microsoft Office Visio indicators that you will measure, analyze and track?
<--- Score

77. What data was collected (past, present, future/ongoing)?
<--- Score

78. Can analysis be automated?
<--- Score

79. Do the benefits outweigh the costs?
<--- Score

80. What causes extra work or rework?
<--- Score

81. Who participated in the data collection for measurements?
<--- Score

82. Have design-to-cost goals been established?
<--- Score

83. What do you measure and why?
<--- Score

84. Are there any easy-to-implement alternatives to Microsoft Office Visio? Sometimes other solutions are available that do not require the cost implications of a full-blown project?
<--- Score

85. What methods are feasible and acceptable to estimate the impact of reforms?
<--- Score

86. Do you aggressively reward and promote the people who have the biggest impact on creating excellent Microsoft Office Visio services/products?
<--- Score

87. Does Microsoft Office Visio systematically track and analyze outcomes for accountability and quality improvement?
<--- Score

88. Is data collected on key measures that were identified?
<--- Score

89. What are your operating costs?
<--- Score

90. What would it cost to replace your technology?
<--- Score

91. Are the business workflows corresponding that only one user would be focused on one set of Aggregate instances at any given time?
<--- Score

92. How will success or failure be measured?
<--- Score

93. What do people want to verify?
<--- Score

94. Are supply costs steady or fluctuating?
<--- Score

95. How would automation impact your organization operation and workflow?
<--- Score

96. What is your decision requirements diagram?
<--- Score

97. Parenthesis. Avoid using parensuchs because they de-emphasize your text, and if what youre writing isnt important, why include it?
<--- Score

98. What has the team done to assure the stability and accuracy of the measurement process?
<--- Score

99. How do you verify your resources?
<--- Score

100. Is data collection planned and executed?
<--- Score

101. Have you found any 'ground fruit' or 'low-hanging fruit' for immediate remedies to the gap in performance?
<--- Score

102. Is there evidence to confirm both the root causes and effects of any problems?
<--- Score

103. Are there any obvious insights can you glean from the data about the severity, cause, or business sector of breaches?
<--- Score

104. Does a Microsoft Office Visio quantification method exist?
<--- Score

105. How are costs allocated?
<--- Score

106. How do you measure success?
<--- Score

107. Does the flowchart show exactly how things are done now?
<--- Score

108. When is Root Cause Analysis Required?

<--- Score

109. How do you prevent mis-estimating cost?
<--- Score

110. Are key measures identified and agreed upon?
<--- Score

111. Have you included everything in your Microsoft Office Visio cost models?
<--- Score

112. How do you focus on what is right -not who is right?
<--- Score

113. What is the difference between a Business Architect and a Business Analyst?
<--- Score

114. Have you made assumptions about the shape of the future, particularly its impact on your customers and competitors?
<--- Score

115. Has your office completed any workflow analysis of mission-related activities?
<--- Score

116. Does the system support escalation workflow approval processes for emergency and priority requests?
<--- Score

117. How can you reduce the costs of obtaining inputs?

<--- Score

118. Is long term and short term variability accounted for?
<--- Score

119. What are your customers expectations and measures?
<--- Score

120. Why do the measurements/indicators matter?
<--- Score

121. What tests verify requirements?
<--- Score

122. How do you measure lifecycle phases?
<--- Score

123. How will costs be allocated?
<--- Score

124. Is the solution cost-effective?
<--- Score

125. Are there measurements based on task performance?
<--- Score

126. Are process variation components displayed/communicated using suitable charts, graphs, plots?
<--- Score

127. Is the flowchart drawn the way participants envision the process or the way it actually works?
<--- Score

128. Might strategic specialization not cause inflexibility and narrow your organizations vision?
<--- Score

129. Was a Microsoft Office Visio charter developed?
<--- Score

130. Analysis (query power and query sophistication): When you are gathering information to make use of that information, how sophisticated are the queries?
<--- Score

131. Have you captured the workflow (which conceptualizes the data inputs, transformations, and analytical steps to achieve the final data output)?
<--- Score

132. How sensitive must the Microsoft Office Visio strategy be to cost?
<--- Score

133. What is the total cost related to deploying Microsoft Office Visio, including any consulting or professional services?
<--- Score

134. What harm might be caused?
<--- Score

135. How can a Microsoft Office Visio test verify your ideas or assumptions?
<--- Score

136. How do you verify and develop ideas and innovations?
<--- Score

137. What is your Microsoft Office Visio quality cost segregation study?
<--- Score

Add up total points for this section:
_____ = Total points for this section

Divided by: _____ (number of statements answered) = _____
Average score for this section

Transfer your score to the Microsoft Office Visio Index at the beginning of the Self-Assessment.

CRITERION #4: ANALYZE:

INTENT: Analyze causes, assumptions
and hypotheses.

In my belief, the answer to this
question is clearly defined:

5 Strongly Agree

4 Agree

3 Neutral

2 Disagree

1 Strongly Disagree

1. What does it mean for a workflow to be data-intensive?
<--- Score

2. Record-keeping requirements flow from the records needed as inputs, outputs, controls and for transformation of a Microsoft Office Visio process, are the records needed as inputs to the Microsoft Office Visio process available?
<--- Score

3. For which processes does workflow system support pay off?

<--- Score

4. Do you provide the ability to establish and implement customized workflows for approval, action, distribution, and routing for managing project/process life cycles?

<--- Score

5. What qualifications are necessary?

<--- Score

6. What were the financial benefits resulting from any 'ground fruit or low-hanging fruit' (quick fixes)?

<--- Score

7. What is the Data Resolution Workflow?

<--- Score

8. Are you able to process documents quickly in a digital workflow?

<--- Score

9. What were the crucial 'moments of truth' on the process map?

<--- Score

10. What is the process to create or change a provisioning workflow?

<--- Score

11. What other jobs or tasks affect the performance of the steps in the Microsoft Office Visio process?

<--- Score

12. How do mission and objectives affect the Microsoft Office Visio processes of your organization?
<--- Score

13. What methods do you use to gather Microsoft Office Visio data?
<--- Score

14. What kind of crime could a potential new hire have committed that would not only not disqualify him/her from being hired by your organization, but would actually indicate that he/she might be a particularly good fit?
<--- Score

15. What parts of the data output by a job are used by downstream jobs in the workflow?
<--- Score

16. What output to create?
<--- Score

17. What would make you, as the reader, respond to an inquiry quickly?
<--- Score

18. Where does the process start?
<--- Score

19. Is the Microsoft Office Visio process severely broken such that a re-design is necessary?
<--- Score

20. Is the gap/opportunity displayed and communicated in financial terms?

<--- Score

21. Workflow Mining: Which Processes can be Rediscovered?
<--- Score

22. How does your organization manage the digitized workflow process?
<--- Score

23. Is full sub-workflow (sub-process) support provided by the system being proposed?
<--- Score

24. What could be the business opportunity for in the future in your opinion?
<--- Score

25. Should you invest in industry-recognized qualifications?
<--- Score

26. How do you measure the operational performance of your key work systems and processes, including productivity, cycle time, and other appropriate measures of process effectiveness, efficiency, and innovation?
<--- Score

27. How do your work systems and key work processes relate to and capitalize on your core competencies?
<--- Score

28. What can your organization hope to achieve by digitizing paper documents through imaging/

capture and electronic forms technologies, and by using workflow and business process management technologies?
<--- Score

29. What data do you want to use?
<--- Score

30. Who is involved with workflow mapping?
<--- Score

31. How is Microsoft Office Visio data gathered?
<--- Score

32. What are the best opportunities for value improvement?
<--- Score

33. Is there a web tool to implement an approval process workflow for audit trail purposes?
<--- Score

34. How does the organization define, manage, and improve its Microsoft Office Visio processes?
<--- Score

35. How many input/output points does it require?
<--- Score

36. Did any additional data need to be collected?
<--- Score

37. Have the problem and goal statements been updated to reflect the additional knowledge gained from the analyze phase?
<--- Score

38. What kind of rough workflow or business process should it implement?

<--- Score

39. Is data and process analysis, root cause analysis and quantifying the gap/opportunity in place?

<--- Score

40. Were Pareto charts (or similar) used to portray the 'heavy hitters' (or key sources of variation)?

<--- Score

41. Is the performance gap determined?

<--- Score

42. Will data miners and data scientist of big data be happy with a tool for data discovery and model building that is completely gui based i.e drag n drop workflow?

<--- Score

43. You have a Workflow or Process Engine

<--- Score

44. An organizationally feasible system request is one that considers the mission, goals and objectives of the organization, key questions are: is the Microsoft Office Visio solution request practical and will it solve a problem or take advantage of an opportunity to achieve company goals?

<--- Score

45. What did the team gain from developing a sub-process map?

<--- Score

46. What qualifications are needed?
<--- Score

47. Has the process workflow been mapped down to the activity or task level, so that all the key elements that drive the performance of the process have been identified and understood?
<--- Score

48. How are you building workflows in the process automation design tool and are you using recorder versus design-based?
<--- Score

49. How do your users manage data and workflow?
<--- Score

50. What tools were used to narrow the list of possible causes?
<--- Score

51. How does your Change Management process area support workflows?
<--- Score

52. Were any designed experiments used to generate additional insight into the data analysis?
<--- Score

53. Do you have a handle on data security/privacy and country laws?
<--- Score

54. Do your contracts/agreements contain data security obligations?

<--- Score

55. What tools were used to generate the list of possible causes?
<--- Score

56. Is all necessary data capture part of the normal developer workflow?
<--- Score

57. Can the ESB orchestrate back-end business processes, including human workflow?
<--- Score

58. Is pre-qualification of suppliers carried out?
<--- Score

59. What is the cost of poor quality as supported by the team's analysis?
<--- Score

60. How many records or what is the size of data handled, while managing business process or workflow?
<--- Score

61. What is the output?
<--- Score

62. What are the revised rough estimates of the financial savings/opportunity for Microsoft Office Visio improvements?
<--- Score

63. Do your employees have the opportunity to do what they do best everyday?

<--- Score

64. Why would you want to store data in a shape?
<--- Score

65. How is the data gathered?
<--- Score

66. Think about some of the processes you undertake within your organization, which do you own?
<--- Score

67. Have any additional benefits been identified that will result from closing all or most of the gaps?
<--- Score

68. What is the Value Stream Mapping?
<--- Score

69. How is the way you as the leader think and process information affecting your organizational culture?
<--- Score

70. How does the purchase order invoice workflow process work?
<--- Score

71. Are current systems consistent with industry best practices for seamless integration of workflow and data?
<--- Score

72. Are Microsoft Office Visio changes recognized early enough to be approved through the regular process?
<--- Score

73. How difficult is it to qualify what Microsoft Office Visio ROI is?

<--- Score

74. How do you promote understanding that opportunity for improvement is not criticism of the status quo, or the people who created the status quo?

<--- Score

75. Has an output goal been set?

<--- Score

76. Security and authentication technologies, allied to event logging, in the cloud computing environment can help auditors as they deal with issues related to workflow were those who entered, approved, changed or otherwise touched data authorized to do so, on an individual, group or role-related basis?

<--- Score

77. What are evaluation criteria for the output?

<--- Score

78. What quality tools were used to get through the analyze phase?

<--- Score

79. What type of sensitive data?

<--- Score

80. What are the services that next generation distributed big data applications and workflows need from networks (san/lan/man/wan)?

<--- Score

81. What are the personnel training and qualifications required?
<--- Score

82. Does the process map influence the outcome of quality improvement work?
<--- Score

83. How do you identify specific Microsoft Office Visio investment opportunities and emerging trends?
<--- Score

84. Do several people in different organizational units assist with the Microsoft Office Visio process?
<--- Score

85. What level of technical ability is required to create new workflow processes, modify existing workflow processes?
<--- Score

86. How often will data be collected for measures?
<--- Score

87. What are the key elements of your Microsoft Office Visio performance improvement system, including your evaluation, organizational learning, and innovation processes?
<--- Score

88. Why Processes and Workflow?
<--- Score

89. Process owner: who is the business owner of the process?

<--- Score

90. How do you become proficient in designing and implementing marketing workflows that drive your organizations business?
<--- Score

91. What does the data say about the performance of the stakeholder process?
<--- Score

92. A compounding model resolution with available relevant data can often provide insight towards a solution methodology; which Microsoft Office Visio models, tools and techniques are necessary?
<--- Score

93. Was a detailed process map created to amplify critical steps of the 'as is' stakeholder process?
<--- Score

94. Change process models and workflows are defined
<--- Score

95. At each step of the process do you ask: What happens next?
<--- Score

96. What are the steps in your deployment process (workflow)?
<--- Score

97. Have you documented information workflows for critical business processes?
<--- Score

98. What training and qualifications will you need?
<--- Score

99. What other organizational variables, such as reward systems or communication systems, affect the performance of this Microsoft Office Visio process?
<--- Score

100. What are the common drivers behind a business process design project?
<--- Score

101. Is there a workflow for paperless processing of applications and approvals?
<--- Score

102. What will drive Microsoft Office Visio change?
<--- Score

103. Was a cause-and-effect diagram used to explore the different types of causes (or sources of variation)?
<--- Score

104. Do you need to provide data to an ecosystem of partners?
<--- Score

105. Does the proposed system provide the ability to embed exception handling processes into the workflow being defined?
<--- Score

106. Where is the data coming from to measure compliance?
<--- Score

107. Are gaps between current performance and the goal performance identified?

<--- Score

108. What is your organizations process which leads to recognition of value generation?

<--- Score

109. Think about the functions involved in your Microsoft Office Visio project, what processes flow from these functions?

<--- Score

110. Do your leaders quickly bounce back from setbacks?

<--- Score

111. Are the workflows and process integrations in place?

<--- Score

112. What metadata creation workflow would you prefer?

<--- Score

113. Are you defining the Key processes of the Business Operating System, or the Key Processes of Product Realization?

<--- Score

114. Process support: how can a project better organizationalize workflow support without adding a bureaucratic burden to the developers?

<--- Score

115. How is financial data updated e.g. via dynamic link, via periodic update, etc.?
<--- Score

116. How can modifications be made to dynamic business rules without changing and migrating workflow processes and custom code?
<--- Score

117. What are the key elements and principles of your business process reengineering (BPR) efforts?
<--- Score

118. What are your Microsoft Office Visio processes?
<--- Score

119. How has the Microsoft Office Visio data been gathered?
<--- Score

120. Did any value-added analysis or 'lean thinking' take place to identify some of the gaps shown on the 'as is' process map?
<--- Score

121. Were there any improvement opportunities identified from the process analysis?
<--- Score

122. How do developers and users of this software decide whether apps qualify as medical devices and which are for health and fitness purposes?
<--- Score

123. How was the detailed process map generated, verified, and validated?

<--- Score

124. What data do you need to collect?
<--- Score

125. Is sensitive data being handled?
<--- Score

126. How should users manage data and workflow?
<--- Score

127. What conclusions were drawn from the team's data collection and analysis? How did the team reach these conclusions?
<--- Score

128. What are your current levels and trends in key measures or indicators of Microsoft Office Visio product and process performance that are important to and directly serve your customers? How do these results compare with the performance of your competitors and other organizations with similar offerings?
<--- Score

129. What are the current procurement processes/ workflows, and strengths and weaknesses?
<--- Score

130. What qualifications do Microsoft Office Visio leaders need?
<--- Score

131. Who owns a data set, which data sets support this business unit, and how can you lock down

data without disrupting workflows?

<--- Score

132. How do you implement and manage your work processes to ensure that they meet design requirements?

<--- Score

133. Is the required Microsoft Office Visio data gathered?

<--- Score

Add up total points for this section:
_____ = Total points for this section

Divided by: _____ (number of statements answered) = _____
Average score for this section

Transfer your score to the Microsoft Office Visio Index at the beginning of the Self-Assessment.

CRITERION #5: IMPROVE:

INTENT: Develop a practical solution.
Innovate, establish and test the
solution and to measure the results.

In my belief, the answer to this
question is clearly defined:

5 Strongly Agree

4 Agree

3 Neutral

2 Disagree

1 Strongly Disagree

1. How do you link measurement and risk?
<--- Score

**2. Do you have an integrated electronic workflow
from method development to method execution?**
<--- Score

3. Who do you report Microsoft Office Visio results to?
<--- Score

4. When you map the key players in your own work and the types/domains of relationships with them, which relationships do you find easy and which challenging, and why?
<--- Score

5. Is there a cost/benefit analysis of optimal solution(s)?
<--- Score

6. Should a workflow be designed and developed as part of this project?
<--- Score

7. Does the solution support the creation of more than one configurable or customizable approval workflow for request intake?
<--- Score

8. Are there any places in the document where it may appear that youre disagreeing with yourself?
<--- Score

9. How will the group know that the solution worked?
<--- Score

10. Can the solution be designed and implemented within an acceptable time period?
<--- Score

11. If you could go back in time five years, what decision would you make differently? What is your best guess as to what decision you're making today you might regret five years from now?
<--- Score

12. What does the 'should be' process map/design look like?
<--- Score

13. How well is the project vision understood by project team members?
<--- Score

14. How do you understand the context?
<--- Score

15. Has the IT department improved workflow alignment to optimize its IT resources?
<--- Score

16. Is a solution implementation plan established, including schedule/work breakdown structure, resources, risk management plan, cost/budget, and control plan?
<--- Score

17. Should your message be a document?
<--- Score

18. What tools were used to tap into the creativity and encourage 'outside the box' thinking?
<--- Score

19. Would examples, details, or graphics help readers to understand?
<--- Score

20. How will the team or the process owner(s) monitor the implementation plan to see that it is working as intended?

<--- Score

21. Is the optimal solution selected based on testing and analysis?
<--- Score

22. What result do you want?
<--- Score

23. How do you improve Microsoft Office Visio service perception, and satisfaction?
<--- Score

24. Are workflows efficient, clearly mapped out, and understood by all staff?
<--- Score

25. What actually has to improve and by how much?
<--- Score

26. What improvements have been achieved?
<--- Score

27. To what extent does management recognize Microsoft Office Visio as a tool to increase the results?
<--- Score

28. How does the team improve its work?
<--- Score

29. Is pilot data collected and analyzed?
<--- Score

30. Why improve in the first place?
<--- Score

31. Examine a document that you have recently written or received. Identify the main point (or claim) and evaluate the effectiveness of the support: Are good types of evidence used?
<--- Score

32. Were any criteria developed to assist the team in testing and evaluating potential solutions?
<--- Score

33. Is there a small-scale pilot for proposed improvement(s)? What conclusions were drawn from the outcomes of a pilot?
<--- Score

34. What is the team's contingency plan for potential problems occurring in implementation?
<--- Score

35. How do the Microsoft Office Visio results compare with the performance of your competitors and other organizations with similar offerings?
<--- Score

36. What resources are required for the improvement efforts?
<--- Score

37. What does the document want you do?
<--- Score

38. What happens when you have developed sophisticated workflows and you need a method to tie them all together?
<--- Score

39. What current systems have to be understood and/ or changed?

<--- Score

40. Who will be using the results of the measurement activities?

<--- Score

41. Do you have a breakdown of how many users will be accessing the system for document management and workflow?

<--- Score

42. What will make it easy for them to understand or act?

<--- Score

43. Risk Identification: What are the possible risk events your organization faces in relation to Microsoft Office Visio?

<--- Score

44. What tools were used to evaluate the potential solutions?

<--- Score

45. Is the measure of success for Microsoft Office Visio understandable to a variety of people?

<--- Score

46. Who controls the risk?

<--- Score

47. How can you improve Microsoft Office Visio?

<--- Score

48. What communications are necessary to support the implementation of the solution?
<--- Score

49. Is a contingency plan established?
<--- Score

50. Is there anything additional that will help the reader understand?
<--- Score

51. Has the team documented the new workflow, with all of the interfaces and dependencies noted?
<--- Score

52. Who are the people involved in developing and implementing Microsoft Office Visio?
<--- Score

53. What attendant changes will need to be made to ensure that the solution is successful?
<--- Score

54. Can you identify any significant risks or exposures to Microsoft Office Visio third- parties (vendors, service providers, alliance partners etc) that concern you?
<--- Score

55. Is there a high likelihood that any recommendations will achieve their intended results?
<--- Score

56. What were the underlying assumptions on the cost-benefit analysis?
<--- Score

57. Do those selected for the Microsoft Office Visio team have a good general understanding of what Microsoft Office Visio is all about?
<--- Score

58. Do the ideas flow from one paragraph to the next in a way that anyone would understand?
<--- Score

59. Risk events: what are the things that could go wrong?
<--- Score

60. Is the implementation plan designed?
<--- Score

61. What tools were most useful during the improve phase?
<--- Score

62. Was a pilot designed for the proposed solution(s)?
<--- Score

63. What is the implementation plan?
<--- Score

64. How are policy decisions made and where?
<--- Score

65. Does the solution provide an approval workflow for vulnerability exceptions?
<--- Score

66. Can workflow be automated for a specific document type and workflow template?

<--- Score

67. Does the goal represent a desired result that can be measured?
<--- Score

68. How do you evaluate workflows?
<--- Score

69. Are the best solutions selected?
<--- Score

70. What is the Microsoft Office Visio's sustainability risk?
<--- Score

71. What results do you want from them?
<--- Score

72. How did the team generate the list of possible solutions?
<--- Score

73. How do you know you have improved workflow?
<--- Score

74. In the past few months, what is the smallest change you have made that has had the biggest positive result? What was it about that small change that produced the large return?
<--- Score

75. A clear result is exact, realistic, and measurable. Do you want to inform your reader?
<--- Score

76. What error proofing will be done to address some of the discrepancies observed in the 'as is' process?
<--- Score

77. Are possible solutions generated and tested?
<--- Score

78. How do you define the solutions' scope?
<--- Score

79. How can you improve your Ethos?
<--- Score

80. Who will be responsible for documenting the Microsoft Office Visio requirements in detail?
<--- Score

81. Describe the design of the pilot and what tests were conducted, if any?
<--- Score

82. Does your solution allow unique user(s) business rules and regulations to be embedded in the workflow?
<--- Score

83. What lessons, if any, from a pilot were incorporated into the design of the full-scale solution?
<--- Score

84. How has workflow changed (improvements or drawbacks)?
<--- Score

85. How will you know that a change is an

improvement?

<--- Score

86. How will you know when its improved?

<--- Score

87. How do you decide how much to remunerate an employee?

<--- Score

88. Are there any constraints (technical, political, cultural, or otherwise) that would inhibit certain solutions?

<--- Score

89. Microsoft Office Visio risk decisions: whose call Is It?

<--- Score

90. How can skill-level changes improve Microsoft Office Visio?

<--- Score

91. Are new and improved process ('should be') maps developed?

<--- Score

92. What tools do you use once you have decided on a Microsoft Office Visio strategy and more importantly how do you choose?

<--- Score

93. What went well, what should change, what can improve?

<--- Score

CRITERION #6: CONTROL:

INTENT: Implement the practical solution. Maintain the performance and correct possible complications.

In my belief, the answer to this question is clearly defined:

5 Strongly Agree

4 Agree

3 Neutral

2 Disagree

1 Strongly Disagree

1. Have new or revised work instructions resulted?
<--- Score

2. Is a response plan established and deployed?
<--- Score

3. How will input, process, and output variables be checked to detect for sub-optimal conditions?
<--- Score

4. Are new process steps, standards, and documentation ingrained into normal operations?
<--- Score

5. How will you measure your QA plan's effectiveness?
<--- Score

6. How will report readings be checked to effectively monitor performance?
<--- Score

7. Who has control over resources?
<--- Score

8. What should the next improvement project be that is related to Microsoft Office Visio?
<--- Score

9. In the case of a Microsoft Office Visio project, the criteria for the audit derive from implementation objectives, an audit of a Microsoft Office Visio project involves assessing whether the recommendations outlined for implementation have been met, can you track that any Microsoft Office Visio project is implemented as planned, and is it working?
<--- Score

10. How will new or emerging customer needs/requirements be checked/communicated to orient the process toward meeting the new specifications and continually reducing variation?
<--- Score

11. What are you attempting to measure/monitor?
<--- Score

12. Are there documented procedures?
<--- Score

13. Does the authority use hyperion planning workflow functionality to control the timing, status and release of budgets and forecasts?
<--- Score

14. Has the Microsoft Office Visio value of standards been quantified?
<--- Score

15. Do you monitor the Microsoft Office Visio decisions made and fine tune them as they evolve?
<--- Score

16. Is knowledge gained on process shared and institutionalized?
<--- Score

17. Are operating procedures consistent?
<--- Score

18. How is change control managed?
<--- Score

19. Does the Microsoft Office Visio performance meet the customer's requirements?
<--- Score

20. What is the best design framework for Microsoft Office Visio organization now that, in a post industrial-age if the top-down, command and control model is no longer relevant?
<--- Score

21. Are marketing campaigns, sales workflow, offline access or territory management capabilities included as standard?
<--- Score

22. What other areas of the group might benefit from the Microsoft Office Visio team's improvements, knowledge, and learning?
<--- Score

23. How do you plan for the cost of succession?
<--- Score

24. Does your business plan include the development of an area in your plant for clean manufacturing?
<--- Score

25. Are suggested corrective/restorative actions indicated on the response plan for known causes to problems that might surface?
<--- Score

26. How do you select, collect, align, and integrate Microsoft Office Visio data and information for tracking daily operations and overall organizational performance, including progress relative to strategic objectives and action plans?
<--- Score

27. How many workflows are you planning to manage?
<--- Score

28. Is there a control plan in place for sustaining

improvements (short and long-term)?
<--- Score

29. Does the response plan contain a definite closed loop continual improvement scheme (e.g., plan-do-check-act)?
<--- Score

30. What quality tools were useful in the control phase?
<--- Score

31. What can you control?
<--- Score

32. What is the recommended frequency of auditing?
<--- Score

33. Is there documentation that will support the successful operation of the improvement?
<--- Score

34. Against what alternative is success being measured?
<--- Score

35. Is a response plan in place for when the input, process, or output measures indicate an 'out-of-control' condition?
<--- Score

36. Is there a transfer of ownership and knowledge to process owner and process team tasked with the responsibilities.
<--- Score

37. How likely is the current Microsoft Office Visio plan to come in on schedule or on budget?
<--- Score

38. How will Microsoft Office Visio decisions be made and monitored?
<--- Score

39. What key inputs and outputs are being measured on an ongoing basis?
<--- Score

40. Does a troubleshooting guide exist or is it needed?
<--- Score

41. What is the control/monitoring plan?
<--- Score

42. Does the core financial system support Messaging API-Workflow standards?
<--- Score

43. What should you measure to verify efficiency gains?
<--- Score

44. Can support from partners be adjusted?
<--- Score

45. Are documented procedures clear and easy to follow for the operators?
<--- Score

46. Who is the Microsoft Office Visio process owner?
<--- Score

47. What is the process for writing the plans?
<--- Score

48. How might the group capture best practices and lessons learned so as to leverage improvements?
<--- Score

49. Does your organizations strategic workforce plan identify your division/office/regions current and future human capital needs and competencies needed to pursue its vision?
<--- Score

50. Are controls in place and consistently applied?
<--- Score

51. Will any special training be provided for results interpretation?
<--- Score

52. What other systems, operations, processes, and infrastructures (hiring practices, staffing, training, incentives/rewards, metrics/dashboards/scorecards, etc.) need updates, additions, changes, or deletions in order to facilitate knowledge transfer and improvements?
<--- Score

53. Is there a standardized process?
<--- Score

54. What are your results for key measures or indicators of the accomplishment of your Microsoft Office Visio strategy and action plans, including building and strengthening core competencies?
<--- Score

55. What is the best process for writing the plans?
<--- Score

56. How do controls support value?
<--- Score

57. Is there a recommended audit plan for routine surveillance inspections of Microsoft Office Visio's gains?
<--- Score

58. Does job training on the documented procedures need to be part of the process team's education and training?
<--- Score

59. Does the core financial system support Workflow Management Coalition standards?
<--- Score

60. Is reporting being used or needed?
<--- Score

61. Does the system allow users to perform workflow activities using a standard web browser such as Internet Explorer and Mozilla Firefox?
<--- Score

62. How will the process owner verify improvement in present and future sigma levels, process capabilities?
<--- Score

63. What are the critical parameters to watch?
<--- Score

64. Is there a documented and implemented monitoring plan?
<--- Score

65. How will the process owner and team be able to hold the gains?
<--- Score

66. Has the improved process and its steps been standardized?
<--- Score

67. How will the day-to-day responsibilities for monitoring and continual improvement be transferred from the improvement team to the process owner?
<--- Score

68. What are the known security controls?
<--- Score

69. Constantly communicate the new direction to staff. HR must rapidly readjust organizational charts, job descriptions, workflow processes, salary levels, performance measurement, etc. Why?
<--- Score

70. Is new knowledge gained imbedded in the response plan?
<--- Score

Add up total points for this section:
_ _ _ _ _ = Total points for this section

Divided by: _ _ _ _ _ _ (number of

statements answered) = _____
Average score for this section

Transfer your score to the Microsoft
Office Visio Index at the beginning of
the Self-Assessment.

CRITERION #7: SUSTAIN:

INTENT: Retain the benefits.

In my belief, the answer to this
question is clearly defined:

5 Strongly Agree

4 Agree

3 Neutral

2 Disagree

1 Strongly Disagree

1. Marketing budgets are tighter, consumers are more skeptical, and social media has changed forever the way we talk about Microsoft Office Visio, how do you gain traction?
<--- Score

2. What do you know that your reader doesnt know?
<--- Score

3. What Microsoft Office Visio skills are most

important?
<--- Score

4. How do you get shapes into a drawing?
<--- Score

5. What is the craziest thing you can do?
<--- Score

6. How will you know that the Microsoft Office Visio project has been successful?
<--- Score

7. What stupid rule would you most like to kill?
<--- Score

8. What facilities and services do Business Incubator tenants share?
<--- Score

9. How likely is it that a customer would recommend your company to a friend or colleague?
<--- Score

10. Is there a transfer workflow in place?
<--- Score

11. Did you make anything up?
<--- Score

12. Are you changing as fast as the world around you?
<--- Score

13. What is your organizations current practice for producing written brochures, reports, and business correspondence?

<--- Score

14. Political -is anyone trying to undermine this project?
<--- Score

15. What is the relative efficiency or practicality of each communication medium?
<--- Score

16. Do you have an incident response workflow in place to remediate any situation?
<--- Score

17. What is the estimated value of the project?
<--- Score

18. Is it too stilted, chatty or bureaucratic?
<--- Score

19. What is your formula for success in Microsoft Office Visio ?
<--- Score

20. What may be the consequences for the performance of an organization if all stakeholders are not consulted regarding Microsoft Office Visio?
<--- Score

21. You have workflow and automated escalation?
<--- Score

22. What are your most important goals for the strategic Microsoft Office Visio objectives?
<--- Score

23. What kinds of situations can you think of in which letters are still the most acceptable way to correspond?
<--- Score

24. How do you automate workflows cutting across the tool boundaries?
<--- Score

25. What is the effect on operations from unscheduled downtime?
<--- Score

26. Does the tool enable automated workflow?
<--- Score

27. What is your workflow software?
<--- Score

28. What is the value add?
<--- Score

29. What are you challenging?
<--- Score

30. What type of correspondence should you create?
<--- Score

31. If you were responsible for initiating and implementing major changes in your organization, what steps might you take to ensure acceptance of those changes?
<--- Score

32. What might motivate the reader of an

unsolicited inquiry to act?
<--- Score

33. How do you know if the system will support the best workflow for the user?
<--- Score

34. How do you build web services based on your workflow model?
<--- Score

35. Why would someone buy your product over your competitors?
<--- Score

36. Do you want to inform?
<--- Score

37. What is the range of capabilities?
<--- Score

38. What might it take to change them?
<--- Score

39. How to reduce potentials for errors during migration of workflow?
<--- Score

40. Are new benefits received and understood?
<--- Score

41. How do you support the workflows in peer production?
<--- Score

42. What about emoticons (faces created out of

keyboard characters. Ex:)?
<--- Score

43. What are you trying to achieve strategically and what hurdles must be met?
<--- Score

44. What are your business writing responsibilities for your job?
<--- Score

45. Have you answered all potential readers questions?
<--- Score

46. What knowledge, skills and characteristics mark a good Microsoft Office Visio project manager?
<--- Score

47. Where and why do you use connectors?
<--- Score

48. Who will be responsible for deciding whether Microsoft Office Visio goes ahead or not after the initial investigations?
<--- Score

49. Is your strategy driving your strategy? Or is the way in which you allocate resources driving your strategy?
<--- Score

50. What happens to workflows?
<--- Score

51. How do you organize and design instructions?

<--- Score

52. Whose voice (department, ethnic group, women, older workers, etc) might you have missed hearing from in your company, and how might you amplify this voice to create positive momentum for your business?
<--- Score

53. Is the reader expecting this?
<--- Score

54. At what moment would you think; Will I get fired?
<--- Score

55. What are strengthsweaknesses of your competitors?
<--- Score

56. If existing applications themselves are subject to change, will the software robots continue to work, or will the rules and workflows break as the application user interfaces change?
<--- Score

57. Does the mes offer escalation management and workflow functions?
<--- Score

58. Do you want to persuade?
<--- Score

59. Who do we want your customers to become?
<--- Score

60. Are you making progress, and are you making

progress as Microsoft Office Visio leaders?
<--- Score

61. When information truly is ubiquitous, when reach and connectivity are completely global, when computing resources are infinite, and when a whole new set of impossibilities are not only possible, but happening, what will that do to your business?
<--- Score

62. How do you get a smooth and continuous workflow?
<--- Score

63. How is security testing integrated with ci/cd workflows?
<--- Score

64. What are you trying to prove to yourself, and how might it be hijacking your life and business success?
<--- Score

65. Who do you want your customers to become?
<--- Score

66. What are you interested in?
<--- Score

67. What time window do you have?
<--- Score

68. Does it allow a configuration that facilitates a productive workflow?
<--- Score

69. Do you use any tools for workflow

management?
<--- Score

70. Is there a workflow component in your system?
<--- Score

71. Who is the reader?
<--- Score

72. How will you insure seamless interoperability of Microsoft Office Visio moving forward?
<--- Score

73. How do you stay inspired?
<--- Score

74. What do you want to accomplish?
<--- Score

75. What happens at your organization when people fail?
<--- Score

76. Would different corporate cultures affect the way you would write a letter of complaint?
<--- Score

77. What are the prerequisites to use the Live Office Interface?
<--- Score

78. How important is Microsoft Office Visio to the user organizations mission?
<--- Score

79. Do you use workflows to track your progress?

<--- Score

80. What are the rules and assumptions your industry operates under? What if the opposite were true?
<--- Score

81. Is it economical; do you have the time and money?
<--- Score

82. For your message to come across well, it helps to consider both sides of the relationship: What exactly do you want out of it, and how will the other person likely respond?
<--- Score

83. What is the usual practice of your organization?
<--- Score

84. Is there a workflow component in the new system?
<--- Score

85. How do you determine the key elements that affect Microsoft Office Visio workforce satisfaction, how are these elements determined for different workforce groups and segments?
<--- Score

86. What difference does it make whether a shape is open or closed?
<--- Score

87. Which Microsoft Office Visio goals are the most important?
<--- Score

88. How do you tailor archive workflow to match business workflow?

<--- Score

89. Have you ever received a correspondence written in the direct or the indirect style that would have been more effective if written in the other style?

<--- Score

90. Was there a point where you got irritated, bored, or annoyed?

<--- Score

91. What are the privacy and security features of the product?

<--- Score

92. What secondary readers may view the message?

<--- Score

93. What is the workflow of the app?

<--- Score

94. Get feedback to tell how youre doing. Is your writing working?

<--- Score

95. Are sentences long and complicated or comfortable length?

<--- Score

96. Do you want to inform your reader?

<--- Score

97. Do you want to persuade your reader?
<--- Score

98. What was the last experiment you ran?
<--- Score

99. Are you comfortable that your boss will be able to give it to his or her boss without any changes?
<--- Score

100. Have benefits been optimized with all key stakeholders?
<--- Score

101. What reasons or reader benefits can you use to support your position?
<--- Score

102. Where did you get confused?
<--- Score

103. What do they already know?
<--- Score

104. Are you using a design thinking approach and integrating Innovation, Microsoft Office Visio Experience, and Brand Value?
<--- Score

105. Is the software device an accessory to a medical device that has a moderate level of concern?
<--- Score

106. What is the appropriate level of automation?

<--- Score

107. Collaborative, content management, workflow tools are in place?
<--- Score

108. What do you want the reader to do?
<--- Score

109. What is the history of the situation?
<--- Score

110. Why use the Common Workflow Language?
<--- Score

111. What are the short and long-term Microsoft Office Visio goals?
<--- Score

112. Think of your Microsoft Office Visio project, what are the main functions?
<--- Score

113. What would you maintain and what would you change?
<--- Score

114. Which workflows cannot move to the public and private clouds?
<--- Score

115. What does your signature ensure?
<--- Score

116. How do you foster the skills, knowledge, talents, attributes, and characteristics you want to have?

<--- Score

117. Can you work with other file types in Visio?
<--- Score

118. What kinds of reactions have you gotten to your writing?
<--- Score

119. Does the workflow include signature capabilities?
<--- Score

120. What are the essentials of internal Microsoft Office Visio management?
<--- Score

121. Does your writing style differ between when you write letters (or perhaps memos) and when you write e-mail?
<--- Score

122. How is tqm effected by workflow?
<--- Score

123. Does the workflow behavior change over time?
<--- Score

124. What does the reader know about the subject?
<--- Score

125. Do Microsoft Office Visio rules make a reasonable demand on a users capabilities?
<--- Score

126. Read your letter from the readers point of view. Is it easy to locate the main message?
<--- Score

127. Are the criteria for selecting recommendations stated?
<--- Score

128. Is every thesis supported?
<--- Score

129. Does your Maximo implementation use any start centers that do not include the workflow inbox?
<--- Score

130. What happens when a new employee joins the organization?
<--- Score

131. How often do you forecast?
<--- Score

132. Is there a logical flow?
<--- Score

133. How and where will they read this?
<--- Score

134. How do you proactively clarify deliverables and Microsoft Office Visio quality expectations?
<--- Score

135. Can you add new custom properties?
<--- Score

136. What are the log files that you can use for troubleshooting?

<--- Score

137. What is a feasible sequencing of reform initiatives over time?

<--- Score

138. How well can you capture the attention of someone receiving your memo?

<--- Score

139. How much time does the reader have to devote to this?

<--- Score

140. When do you use a graphic?

<--- Score

141. What type of space will express your offices vision?

<--- Score

142. When do you think it is best to communicate in writing?

<--- Score

143. What projects are going on in the organization today, and what resources are those projects using from the resource pools?

<--- Score

144. What is something you believe that nearly no one agrees with you on?

<--- Score

145. What hurdles might block your message?
<--- Score

146. When can you take the human out of the workflow?
<--- Score

147. Who agrees with you?
<--- Score

148. Are all key stakeholders present at all Structured Walkthroughs?
<--- Score

149. When do you use a table?
<--- Score

150. Have you ever had to correspond with a person from another culture?
<--- Score

151. What information would you be sure to include?
<--- Score

152. What goals did you miss?
<--- Score

153. How can you use your attitude when writing an unsolicited inquiry?
<--- Score

154. Who are your readers?
<--- Score

155. Do you have the right capabilities and capacities?
<--- Score

156. The vision: where do you want to be in terms of your organizational form?
<--- Score

157. Which functions and people interact with the supplier and or customer?
<--- Score

158. Check your tone. Is it too stilted, chatty or bureaucratic?
<--- Score

159. What is your relationship with your reader?
<--- Score

160. If strategies are visions, then what role does seeing play in strategic thinking?
<--- Score

161. How do you accomplish your long range Microsoft Office Visio goals?
<--- Score

162. How will you motivate the stakeholders with the least vested interest?
<--- Score

163. What do your reports reflect?
<--- Score

164. How does Microsoft Office Visio integrate with other stakeholder initiatives?
<--- Score

165. If your company went out of business tomorrow, would anyone who doesn't get a paycheck here care?
<--- Score

166. Is you everyone in general or the specific person reading the statement?
<--- Score

167. Why is Microsoft Office Visio important for you now?
<--- Score

168. What one word do you want to own in the minds of your customers, employees, and partners?
<--- Score

169. What happens when the text is too difficult?
<--- Score

170. Purpose for reading?
<--- Score

171. How do you create buy-in?
<--- Score

172. Why should you adopt a Microsoft Office Visio framework?
<--- Score

173. Avoid simply sending a forwarded chain of messages with a What are your thoughts?
<--- Score

174. Each day, how much time do you spend writing at work?

<--- Score

175. Before you send an email message, ask yourself, would I say this to this person s face?
<--- Score

176. What is the funding source for this project?
<--- Score

177. Who are the major competitors in this industry?
<--- Score

178. Iwhat information must your message include?
<--- Score

179. Is the workflow enabled with end to end interaction that includes follow ups?
<--- Score

180. What are the challenges?
<--- Score

181. How does this connect to the workplace?
<--- Score

182. Is your writing foggy?
<--- Score

183. What are the most significant application security testing challenges inherent in continuous integration/continuous delivery (CI/CD) workflows?
<--- Score

184. Is a graphical, drag & drop, point & click design workflow modeling environment provided?
<--- Score

185. Why will customers want to buy your organizations products/services?
<--- Score

186. How can you negotiate Microsoft Office Visio successfully with a stubborn boss, an irate client, or a deceitful coworker?
<--- Score

187. Are the words precise?
<--- Score

188. Is the workflow system working normally?
<--- Score

189. How are tasks implemented on different clouds and how do you maintain a smooth workflow for your organization?
<--- Score

190. Who is responsible for Microsoft Office Visio?
<--- Score

191. How do you compare with your competitors?
<--- Score

192. Does the workflow include E-signature capabilities?
<--- Score

193. How ambitious can the future vision be?
<--- Score

194. Is a forms design function for creating interactive electronic forms, to be accessed by workflow participants, provided by the proposed system?
<--- Score

195. Which individuals, teams or departments will be involved in Microsoft Office Visio?
<--- Score

196. What has been the growth rate for the BPA tool market during the past three to four years?
<--- Score

197. To create parallel systems or custom workflows?
<--- Score

198. How will you ensure you get what you expected?
<--- Score

199. What is the overall talent health of your organization as a whole at senior levels, and for each organization reporting to a member of the Senior Leadership Team?
<--- Score

200. What is your purpose?
<--- Score

201. What can a Workflow Management System do?
<--- Score

202. What is your approval workflow?

<--- Score

203. What are current Microsoft Office Visio paradigms?
<--- Score

204. What are strengths/weaknesses of your competitors?
<--- Score

205. What are the principal concerns and responsibilities of the reader?
<--- Score

206. What are your purposes in writing?
<--- Score

207. What happens if you group such shapes and then assign the group to another different layer?
<--- Score

208. What Microsoft Office Visio modifications can you make work for you?
<--- Score

209. How do you assess the Microsoft Office Visio pitfalls that are inherent in implementing it?
<--- Score

210. How would the system fit in with the users normal workflow or daily activities?
<--- Score

211. How does your pricing compare to your competitors?
<--- Score

212. How do you configure the workflow?
<--- Score

213. Who, on the executive team or the board, has spoken to a customer recently?
<--- Score

214. Do you have a GroupWare and Workflow system?
<--- Score

215. Is the assertion clearly stated?
<--- Score

216. What types of claims can you make?
<--- Score

217. If the reader were to forget everything else, what one main message do I want him or her to remember?
<--- Score

218. Is there a simpler way to convey the message?
<--- Score

219. What would you do during prewriting, drafting, revising, and refining?
<--- Score

220. What makes your business different from the competition?
<--- Score

221. Do you have good references?
<--- Score

222. How do you profile your reader(s)?
<--- Score

223. Is this something that is going to automate a part of your workflow or make your life easier?
<--- Score

224. What is the urgency to deploy mitigation actions (patches or work-arounds)?
<--- Score

225. Do you have the right people on the bus?
<--- Score

226. What is the current status of cross-functional communication between the functions included in the category management workflow?
<--- Score

227. In a project to restructure Microsoft Office Visio outcomes, which stakeholders would you involve?
<--- Score

228. What would you recommend your friend do if he/ she were facing this dilemma?
<--- Score

229. Do you have an incident response workflow in place to remediate a situation?
<--- Score

230. What is the source of the strategies for Microsoft Office Visio strengthening and reform?
<--- Score

231. What trophy do you want on your mantle?
<--- Score

232. Do you have past Microsoft Office Visio successes?
<--- Score

233. What secondary readers are there?
<--- Score

234. How to manage workflows and projects, that are inherently distributed outside your organizational structure?
<--- Score

235. How might your impression of a company affect the way you write this letter?
<--- Score

236. Does this program contribute to a wide range of Vision objectives?
<--- Score

237. Is a Microsoft Office Visio team work effort in place?
<--- Score

238. Did it take a long time to write?
<--- Score

239. Do you think Microsoft Office Visio accomplishes the goals you expect it to accomplish?
<--- Score

240. Is the impact that Microsoft Office Visio has shown?

<--- Score

241. Which workflows should you account for in your integration?
<--- Score

242. Do you know who is a friend or a foe?
<--- Score

243. How familiar with the topic is this person?
<--- Score

244. Who exactly is your reader?
<--- Score

245. Do you use the Service Catalog and workflow tools to support CSI activities?
<--- Score

246. Which workflows can move to the public and private clouds, respectfully?
<--- Score

247. Do not assume. What do you know that your reader does not know?
<--- Score

248. Who is responsible for errors?
<--- Score

249. Can you maintain your growth without detracting from the factors that have contributed to your success?
<--- Score

250. Why do and why don't your customers like your

organization?

<--- Score

251. Is someone else communicating the same information?

<--- Score

252. How do you experience your workflow to match the business its workflow?

<--- Score

253. What is the ideal tool for a casual business user?

<--- Score

254. How will the reader react to your main message: Receptive?

<--- Score

255. What does the workflow looks like?

<--- Score

256. Is maximizing Microsoft Office Visio protection the same as minimizing Microsoft Office Visio loss?

<--- Score

257. Why is the path of workflow essential to consider in health laboratories?

<--- Score

258. How complicated are workflows?

<--- Score

259. Who will have fun reading it?

<--- Score

260. What are specific Microsoft Office Visio rules to follow?

<--- Score

261. Who are your primary and secondary audiences?

<--- Score

262. What happens if you do not have enough funding?

<--- Score

263. Is non-conformance management workflow-supported?

<--- Score

264. How do you engage the workforce, in addition to satisfying them?

<--- Score

265. Does your organization have a clear vision and strategy?

<--- Score

266. How might an international audience for a letter affect the way you write it, or would it?

<--- Score

267. What information might you exclude?

<--- Score

268. Have you addressed all the changes requested by others?

<--- Score

269. How do you visualize the teams workflow?

<--- Score

270. How much do my top tier suppliers rely on my business?

<--- Score

271. Would you rather sell to knowledgeable and informed customers or to uninformed customers?

<--- Score

272. Is Microsoft Office Visio dependent on the successful delivery of a current project?

<--- Score

273. Which workflows can move to the public and private clouds?

<--- Score

274. How do you deal with Microsoft Office Visio changes?

<--- Score

275. When closing a call or other type of customer transaction, are employees expected to thank customers for their business?

<--- Score

276. How specific should you be when referring the reader to additional sources?

<--- Score

277. What would you think if you received it?

<--- Score

278. What are your readers communication characteristics?

<--- Score

279. What is the implication if you dont?
<--- Score

280. How many configurable workflow business rule templates are available out-of-the-box with your system?
<--- Score

281. Translation Workflow Make or Buy?
<--- Score

282. What new services of functionality will be implemented next with Microsoft Office Visio ?
<--- Score

283. Are the workflows simple (submit/ review/ approve) or complex (ideation through archive)?
<--- Score

284. Who else should you help?
<--- Score

285. What was the vision of the founder?
<--- Score

286. Are there any ways today in which paper correspondence would be inappropriate, in other words, in which only e-mail is appropriate?
<--- Score

287. How would you describe the workflow?
<--- Score

288. What is your Microsoft Office Visio strategy?

<--- Score

289. When deadlines on several writing tasks are rapidly approaching, do you feel under stress?
<--- Score

290. Do you have enough freaky customers in your portfolio pushing you to the limit day in and day out?
<--- Score

291. What could happen if you do not do it?
<--- Score

292. Are your responses positive or negative?
<--- Score

293. If you had to leave your organization for a year and the only communication you could have with employees/colleagues was a single paragraph, what would you write?
<--- Score

294. Is it clear what you want the reader to do or know?
<--- Score

295. What elements of your office or role are leadership tasks building or communicating vision, soliciting support of others to work toward your vision?
<--- Score

296. Draft a closing that indicates action or follow-up. What is revising?
<--- Score

297. Can you elaborate on the notification/ alerting workflows involving buildings, building occupants, and addresses of recipients?
<--- Score

298. How can you write for both skimmers and skeptics at the same time?
<--- Score

299. Disruption of established and effective workflows?
<--- Score

300. What would have to be true for the option on the table to be the best possible choice?
<--- Score

301. Who is (are) your audiences?
<--- Score

302. How do you design tools that guide pedagogically sound design?
<--- Score

303. How do you maintain Microsoft Office Visio's Integrity?
<--- Score

304. Why should people listen to you?
<--- Score

305. Why a new workflow?
<--- Score

306. What is your rhetorical situation?
<--- Score

307. Do you think you know, or do you know you know ?

<--- Score

308. Is there a sufficient level of written operational guidance to ensure day-to-day compliance?

<--- Score

309. Are there special concerns or strong views about the subject?

<--- Score

310. How many configurable workflow actions are available out-of-the-box with your system?

<--- Score

311. What would you do if you didnt know the answers to the readers questions?

<--- Score

312. What is the point of having a style?

<--- Score

313. Will your boss have to think?

<--- Score

314. How can you tell if your board is using Simplified Workflow?

<--- Score

315. How will an unsolicited inquiry differ from a solicited inquiry in terms of tone, style, and organization?

<--- Score

316. What do we do when new problems arise?
<--- Score

317. When is it time to retire the old system and redesign or upgrade to a newer system?
<--- Score

318. What objections can you expect your reader(s) to have?
<--- Score

319. What workflows do you want to automate?
<--- Score

320. How do you know which Visio is right for you?
<--- Score

321. Who are your existing competitors?
<--- Score

322. What is the purpose of drawing scale?
<--- Score

323. How will your organizations vision of being the best organization in your organization prevail?
<--- Score

324. Does the workflow support and include any web services for integrations?
<--- Score

325. How can you best support your conclusions?
<--- Score

326. What are the top 3 things at the forefront of your

Microsoft Office Visio agendas for the next 3 years?
<--- Score

327. How can you become more high-tech but still be high touch?
<--- Score

328. Are there queues or buffers in your workflow that arent represented on the board?
<--- Score

329. Do you see more potential in people than they do in themselves?
<--- Score

330. What makes a claim strong?
<--- Score

331. Is active voice used?
<--- Score

332. When should application security testing be integrated with CI/CD workflows?
<--- Score

333. Have new benefits been realized?
<--- Score

334. What level of product support do you receive once the product is purchased?
<--- Score

335. Has your organization built compliance partnerships and applied programs globally?
<--- Score

336. How much contingency will be available in the budget?

<--- Score

337. How do you set Microsoft Office Visio stretch targets and how do you get people to not only participate in setting these stretch targets but also that they strive to achieve these?

<--- Score

338. How do your records fit into your current workflow?

<--- Score

339. Does this project support your organization vision?

<--- Score

340. Does this project have any dependencies on other initiatives or vice versa?

<--- Score

341. Did your employees make progress today?

<--- Score

342. What can workflow management do for you?

<--- Score

343. How will you use workflows?

<--- Score

344. Is there any existing Microsoft Office Visio governance structure?

<--- Score

345. What can you do with a background?

<--- Score

346. Who is responsible for application security testing in DevOps workflows?
<--- Score

347. What do you believe works well in your writing?
<--- Score

348. How do you organize persuasive messages?
<--- Score

349. What do you like to think about and talk about?
<--- Score

350. Are there any activities that you can take off your to do list?
<--- Score

351. What workflows do you automate?
<--- Score

352. Who have you, as a company, historically been when you've been at your best?
<--- Score

353. Would you use corresponding workflows in a future project?
<--- Score

354. Is there a list of the workflows that are expected to be delivered?
<--- Score

355. When do you add some excitement to your shapes by making them patterned and colorful with shadows?
<--- Score

356. How do you know if you are successful?
<--- Score

357. Were lessons learned captured and communicated?
<--- Score

358. Is a Microsoft Office Visio breakthrough on the horizon?
<--- Score

Add up total points for this section:
_ _ _ _ _ = Total points for this section

Divided by: _ _ _ _ _ _ (number of statements answered) = _ _ _ _ _ _ Average score for this section

Transfer your score to the Microsoft Office Visio Index at the beginning of the Self-Assessment.

Microsoft Office Visio and Managing Projects, Criteria for Project Managers:

1.0 Initiating Process Group: Microsoft Office Visio

1. Did the Microsoft Office Visio project team have the right skills?

2. During which stage of Risk planning are risks prioritized based on probability and impact?

3. What communication items need improvement?

4. Although the Microsoft Office Visio project manager does not directly manage procurement and contracting activities, who does manage procurement and contracting activities in your organization then if not the PM?

5. Were decisions made in a timely manner?

6. How should needs be met?

7. Are you properly tracking the progress of the Microsoft Office Visio project and communicating the status to stakeholders?

8. What are the pressing issues of the hour?

9. How is each deliverable reviewed, verified, and validated?

10. What are the inputs required to produce the deliverables?

11. How will you know you did it?

12. At which cmmi level are software processes documented, standardized, and integrated into a standard to-be practiced process for your organization?

13. Who does what?

14. What are the overarching issues of your organization?

15. Are you just doing busywork to pass the time?

16. In which Microsoft Office Visio project management process group is the detailed Microsoft Office Visio project budget created?

17. Who supports, improves, and oversees standardized processes related to the Microsoft Office Visio projects program?

18. Information sharing?

19. Where must it be done?

20. Have the stakeholders identified all individual requirements pertaining to business process?

1.1 Project Charter: Microsoft Office Visio

21. How high should you set your goals?

22. Review the general mission What system will be affected by the improvement efforts?

23. What are you trying to accomplish?

24. Customer benefits: what customer requirements does this Microsoft Office Visio project address?

25. When is a charter needed?

26. What are the assigned resources?

27. Where and how does the team fit within your organization structure?

28. Are you building in-house ?

29. Market – identify products market, including whether it is outside of the objective: what is the purpose of the program or Microsoft Office Visio project?

30. How will you know that a change is an improvement?

31. Are there special technology requirements?

32. What is the justification?

33. Fit with other Products Compliments – Cannibalizes?

34. Name and describe the elements that deal with providing the detail?

35. Why have you chosen the aim you have set forth?

36. What is the business need?

37. What material?

38. Run it as as a startup?

39. Why is a Microsoft Office Visio project Charter used?

40. Who manages integration?

1.2 Stakeholder Register: Microsoft Office Visio

41. How should employers make voices heard?

42. What & Why?

43. Who are the stakeholders?

44. How much influence do they have on the Microsoft Office Visio project?

45. What is the power of the stakeholder?

46. What opportunities exist to provide communications?

47. How big is the gap?

48. What are the major Microsoft Office Visio project milestones requiring communications or providing communications opportunities?

49. Is your organization ready for change?

50. How will reports be created?

51. Who is managing stakeholder engagement?

52. Who wants to talk about Security?

1.3 Stakeholder Analysis Matrix: Microsoft Office Visio

53. Inoculations or payment to receive them?

54. Cashflow, start-up cash-drain?

55. What is social & public accountability ?

56. Participatory approach: how will key stakeholders participate in the Microsoft Office Visio project?

57. Location and geographical?

58. How do customers express needs?

59. Industry or lifestyle trends?

60. How will the Microsoft Office Visio project benefit them?

61. What organizational arrangements are planned to ensure the Microsoft Office Visio project achieves its social development outcomes?

62. Why involve the stakeholder?

63. What is the stakeholders power and status in relation to the Microsoft Office Visio project?

64. What is your Risk Management?

65. Why do you need to manage Microsoft Office Visio

project Risk?

66. Would it be fair to say that cost is a controlling criteria?

67. Geographical, export, import?

68. What obstacles does your organization face?

69. Guiding question: what is the issue at stake?

70. Who will be affected by the Microsoft Office Visio project?

71. How are the threatened Microsoft Office Visio project targets being used?

72. Who has the power to influence the outcomes of the work?

2.0 Planning Process Group: Microsoft Office Visio

73. Who are the Microsoft Office Visio project stakeholders?

74. Are there efficient coordination mechanisms to avoid overloading the counterparts, participating stakeholders?

75. What is the NEXT thing to do?

76. Why do it Microsoft Office Visio projects fail?

77. What are the different approaches to building the WBS?

78. Will you be replaced?

79. What should you do next?

80. First of all, should any action be taken?

81. Does the program have follow-up mechanisms (to verify the quality of the products, punctuality of delivery, etc.) to measure progress in the achievement of the envisaged results?

82. How are the principles of aid effectiveness (ownership, alignment, management for development results and mutual responsibility) being applied in the Microsoft Office Visio project?

83. In which Microsoft Office Visio project management process group is the detailed Microsoft Office Visio project budget created?

84. What is involved in Microsoft Office Visio project scope management, and why is good Microsoft Office Visio project scope management so important on information technology Microsoft Office Visio projects?

85. How do you integrate Microsoft Office Visio project Planning with the Iterative/Evolutionary SDLC?

86. What factors are contributing to progress or delay in the achievement of products and results?

87. When will the Microsoft Office Visio project be done?

88. What do you need to do?

89. What is a Software Development Life Cycle (SDLC)?

90. If task x starts two days late, what is the effect on the Microsoft Office Visio project end date?

91. To what extent have the target population and participants made the activities own, taking an active role in it?

92. If a task is partitionable, is this a sufficient condition to reduce the Microsoft Office Visio project duration?

2.1 Project Management Plan: Microsoft Office Visio

93. Why Change?

94. Are the existing and future without-plan conditions reasonable and appropriate?

95. Is the engineering content at a feasibility level-of-detail, and is it sufficiently complete, to provide an adequate basis for the baseline cost estimate?

96. What are the training needs?

97. Is the appropriate plan selected based on your organizations objectives and evaluation criteria expressed in Principles and Guidelines policies?

98. What is risk management?

99. Are there any client staffing expectations?

100. What does management expect of PMs?

101. Development trends and opportunities. What if the positive direction and vision of your organization causes expected trends to change?

102. What went right?

103. Is there an incremental analysis/cost effectiveness analysis of proposed mitigation features based on an approved method and using an accepted

model?

104. If the Microsoft Office Visio project is complex or scope is specialized, do you have appropriate and/or qualified staff available to perform the tasks?

105. What goes into your Microsoft Office Visio project Charter?

106. What would you do differently?

107. What worked well?

108. Is the budget realistic?

109. Does the implementation plan have an appropriate division of responsibilities?

110. What data/reports/tools/etc. do program managers need?

111. When is the Microsoft Office Visio project management plan created?

112. Will you add a schedule and diagram?

2.2 Scope Management Plan: Microsoft Office Visio

113. Is there general agreement & acceptance of the current status and progress of the Microsoft Office Visio project?

114. Have Microsoft Office Visio project team accountabilities & responsibilities been clearly defined?

115. Do all stakeholders know how to access this repository and where to find the Microsoft Office Visio project documentation?

116. Have all involved Microsoft Office Visio project stakeholders and work groups committed to the Microsoft Office Visio project?

117. Were Microsoft Office Visio project team members involved in detailed estimating and scheduling?

118. Has the Microsoft Office Visio project approach and development strategy of the Microsoft Office Visio project been defined, documented and accepted by the appropriate stakeholders?

119. What problem is being solved by delivering this Microsoft Office Visio project?

120. Function of the configuration control board?

121. Are target dates established for each milestone deliverable?

122. Are schedule deliverables actually delivered?

123. Pop quiz – which are the same inputs as in scope planning?

124. What are the Quality Assurance overheads?

125. Describe the process for accepting the Microsoft Office Visio project deliverables. Will the Microsoft Office Visio project deliverables become accepted in writing?

126. Timeline and milestones?

127. Have the scope, objectives, costs, benefits and impacts been communicated to all involved and/or impacted stakeholders and work groups?

128. Does the business case include how the Microsoft Office Visio project aligns with your organizations strategic goals & objectives?

129. Has the scope management document been updated and distributed to help prevent scope creep?

130. Does the quality assurance process provide objective verification of adherence to applicable standards, procedures & requirements?

131. Are software metrics formally captured, analyzed and used as a basis for other Microsoft Office Visio project estimates?

132. Is a pmo (Microsoft Office Visio project management office) in place and provide oversight to the Microsoft Office Visio project?

2.3 Requirements Management Plan: Microsoft Office Visio

133. Is requirements work dependent on any other specific Microsoft Office Visio project or non-Microsoft Office Visio project activities (e.g. funding, approvals, procurement)?

134. When and how will a requirements baseline be established in this Microsoft Office Visio project?

135. Controlling Microsoft Office Visio project requirements involves monitoring the status of the Microsoft Office Visio project requirements and managing changes to the requirements. Who is responsible for monitoring and tracking the Microsoft Office Visio project requirements?

136. Do you expect stakeholders to be cooperative?

137. What is the earliest finish date for this Microsoft Office Visio project if it is scheduled to start on ...?

138. Is it new or replacing an existing business system or process?

139. Define the help desk model. who will take full responsibility?

140. Did you provide clear and concise specifications?

141. Who is responsible for monitoring and tracking the Microsoft Office Visio project requirements?

142. How will the information be distributed?

143. How will bidders price evaluations be done, by deliverables, phases, or in a big bang?

144. Is the system software (non-operating system) new to the IT Microsoft Office Visio project team?

145. Are all the stakeholders ready for the transition into the user community?

146. Is there formal agreement on who has authority to request a change in requirements?

147. Subject to change control?

148. Did you use declarative statements?

149. What cost metrics will be used?

150. Have stakeholders been instructed in the Change Control process?

151. Will you document changes to requirements?

2.4 Requirements Documentation: Microsoft Office Visio

152. Is new technology needed?

153. If applicable; are there issues linked with the fact that this is an offshore Microsoft Office Visio project?

154. What happens when requirements are wrong?

155. Basic work/business process; high-level, what is being touched?

156. Are there any requirements conflicts?

157. How will they be documented / shared?

158. Has requirements gathering uncovered information that would necessitate changes?

159. Can the requirements be checked?

160. What variations exist for a process?

161. What kind of entity is a problem ?

162. What are the acceptance criteria?

163. How do you know when a Requirement is accurate enough?

164. Does the system provide the functions which best support the customers needs?

165. What are current process problems?

166. Is the requirement properly understood?

167. What is the risk associated with cost and schedule?

168. Validity. does the system provide the functions which best support the customers needs?

169. Do technical resources exist?

170. What is your Elevator Speech?

171. Does your organization restrict technical alternatives?

2.5 Requirements Traceability Matrix: Microsoft Office Visio

172. How will it affect the stakeholders personally in career?

173. Why do you manage scope?

174. What is the WBS?

175. Do you have a clear understanding of all subcontracts in place?

176. How do you manage scope?

177. How small is small enough?

178. Why use a WBS?

179. What are the chronologies, contingencies, consequences, criteria?

180. Is there a requirements traceability process in place?

181. Will you use a Requirements Traceability Matrix?

182. Describe the process for approving requirements so they can be added to the traceability matrix and Microsoft Office Visio project work can be performed. Will the Microsoft Office Visio project requirements become approved in writing?

183. What percentage of Microsoft Office Visio projects are producing traceability matrices between requirements and other work products?

2.6 Project Scope Statement: Microsoft Office Visio

184. Will the qa related information be reported regularly as part of the status reporting mechanisms?

185. Will the Microsoft Office Visio project risks be managed according to the Microsoft Office Visio projects risk management process?

186. If there is an independent oversight contractor, have they signed off on the Microsoft Office Visio project Plan?

187. Is the change control process documented and on file?

188. Write a brief purpose statement for this Microsoft Office Visio project. Include a business justification statement. What is the product of this Microsoft Office Visio project?

189. Are the meetings set up to have assigned note takers that will add action/issues to the issue list?

190. Are there completion/verification criteria defined for each task producing an output?

191. What is change?

192. Microsoft Office Visio project lead, team lead, solution architect?

193. Will there be a Change Control Process in place?

194. Is the Microsoft Office Visio project manager qualified and experienced in Microsoft Office Visio project management?

195. What process would you recommend for creating the Microsoft Office Visio project scope statement?

196. What are the defined meeting materials?

197. Elements of scope management that deal with concept development ?

198. What should you drop in order to add something new?

199. What actions will be taken to mitigate the risk?

200. Is the plan for Microsoft Office Visio project resources adequate?

201. How will you verify the accuracy of the work of the Microsoft Office Visio project, and what constitutes acceptance of the deliverables?

202. Once its defined, what is the stability of the Microsoft Office Visio project scope?

203. Are there adequate Microsoft Office Visio project control systems?

2.7 Assumption and Constraint Log: Microsoft Office Visio

204. When can log be discarded?

205. Does the document/deliverable meet general requirements (for example, statement of work) for all deliverables?

206. How are new requirements or changes to requirements identified?

207. Does the system design reflect the requirements?

208. Are there procedures in place to effectively manage interdependencies with other Microsoft Office Visio projects / systems?

209. Is there documentation of system capability requirements, data requirements, environment requirements, security requirements, and computer and hardware requirements?

210. What weaknesses do you have?

211. Are there processes in place to ensure that all the terms and code concepts have been documented consistently?

212. Does a specific action and/or state that is known to violate security policy occur?

213. Are formal code reviews conducted?

214. What does an audit system look like?

215. What strengths do you have?

216. If it is out of compliance, should the process be amended or should the Plan be amended?

217. Was the document/deliverable developed per the appropriate or required standards (for example, Institute of Electrical and Electronics Engineers standards)?

218. Do the requirements meet the standards of correctness, completeness, consistency, accuracy, and readability?

219. How can constraints be violated?

220. Security analysis has access to information that is sanitized?

221. Does the traceability documentation describe the tool and/or mechanism to be used to capture traceability throughout the life cycle?

2.8 Work Breakdown Structure: Microsoft Office Visio

222. Why would you develop a Work Breakdown Structure?

223. How many levels?

224. How big is a work-package?

225. How much detail?

226. Who has to do it?

227. Is it a change in scope?

228. When do you stop?

229. When does it have to be done?

230. How far down?

231. What is the probability that the Microsoft Office Visio project duration will exceed xx weeks?

232. Why is it useful?

233. Can you make it?

234. Do you need another level?

235. Where does it take place?

236. When would you develop a Work Breakdown
Structure?

2.9 WBS Dictionary: Microsoft Office Visio

237. Is authorization of budgets in excess of the contract budget base controlled formally and done with the full knowledge and recognition of the procuring activity?

238. Are authorized changes being incorporated in a timely manner?

239. Does the contractors system provide for accurate cost accumulation and assignment to control accounts in a manner consistent with the budgets using recognized acceptable costing techniques?

240. Are detailed work packages planned as far in advance as practicable?

241. Are records maintained to show full accountability for all material purchased for the contract, including the residual inventory?

242. Changes in the overhead pool and/or organization structures?

243. Does the contractors system include procedures for measuring the performance of critical subcontractors?

244. Are the procedures for identifying indirect costs to incurring organizations, indirect cost pools, and allocating the costs from the pools to the contracts

formally documented?

245. Are control accounts opened and closed based on the start and completion of work contained therein?

246. Do work packages consist of discrete tasks which are adequately described?

247. Does the accounting system provide a basis for auditing records of direct costs chargeable to the contract?

248. Are the bases and rates for allocating costs from each indirect pool consistently applied?

249. Identify and isolate causes of favorable and unfavorable cost and schedule variances?

250. Are retroactive changes to budgets for completed work specifically prohibited in an established procedure, and is this procedure adhered to?

251. Are records maintained to show how undistributed budgets are controlled?

252. Does the contractors system provide unit costs, equivalent unit or lot costs in terms of labor, material, other direct, and indirect costs?

253. Are time-phased budgets established for planning and control of level of effort activity by category of resource; for example, type of manpower and/or material?

254. Are the rates for allocating costs from each indirect cost pool to contracts updated as necessary to ensure a realistic monthly allocation of indirect costs without significant year-end adjustments?

255. Changes in the nature of the overhead requirements?

2.10 Schedule Management Plan: Microsoft Office Visio

256. Have adequate resources been provided by management to ensure Microsoft Office Visio project success?

257. Is a process for scheduling and reporting defined, including forms and formats?

258. Are the Microsoft Office Visio project team members located locally to the users/stakeholders?

259. Is there any form of automated support for Issues Management?

260. Is there an issues management plan in place?

261. Has a capability assessment been conducted?

262. Have stakeholder accountabilities & responsibilities been clearly defined?

263. Are the appropriate IT resources adequate to meet planned commitments?

264. What date will the task finish?

265. Does the detailed work plan match the complexity of tasks with the capabilities of personnel?

266. Are there any activities or deliverables being added or gold-plated that could be dropped or scaled

back without falling short of the original requirement?

267. Is the steering committee active in Microsoft Office Visio project oversight?

268. Sensitivity analysis?

269. Is the schedule updated on a periodic basis?

270. Is the schedule vertically and horizontally traceable?

271. Are all vendor contracts closed out?

272. Do all stakeholders know how to access this repository and where to find the Microsoft Office Visio project documentation?

273. Can be realistically shortened (the duration of subsequent tasks)?

274. Is current scope of the Microsoft Office Visio project substantially different than that originally defined?

275. Are the key elements of a Microsoft Office Visio project Charter present?

2.11 Activity List: Microsoft Office Visio

276. What did not go as well?

277. What is your organizations history in doing similar activities?

278. Should you include sub-activities?

279. Can you determine the activity that must finish, before this activity can start?

280. What went wrong?

281. For other activities, how much delay can be tolerated?

282. Is there anything planned that does not need to be here?

283. When do the individual activities need to start and finish?

284. What went well?

285. What are the critical bottleneck activities?

286. How should ongoing costs be monitored to try to keep the Microsoft Office Visio project within budget?

287. Is infrastructure setup part of your Microsoft Office Visio project?

288. What is the probability the Microsoft Office Visio project can be completed in xx weeks?

289. What is the total time required to complete the Microsoft Office Visio project if no delays occur?

290. How do you determine the late start (LS) for each activity?

291. How will it be performed?

292. How difficult will it be to do specific activities on this Microsoft Office Visio project?

293. Are the required resources available or need to be acquired?

294. How can the Microsoft Office Visio project be displayed graphically to better visualize the activities?

2.12 Activity Attributes: Microsoft Office Visio

295. How many resources do you need to complete the work scope within a limit of X number of days?

296. How difficult will it be to complete specific activities on this Microsoft Office Visio project?

297. Activity: what is In the Bag?

298. Activity: fair or not fair?

299. Would you consider either of corresponding activities an outlier?

300. Have constraints been applied to the start and finish milestones for the phases?

301. Which method produces the more accurate cost assignment?

302. How many days do you need to complete the work scope with a limit of X number of resources?

303. What is the general pattern here?

304. What conclusions/generalizations can you draw from this?

305. How else could the items be grouped?

306. What activity do you think you should spend the

most time on?

307. How difficult will it be to do specific activities on this Microsoft Office Visio project?

308. Were there other ways you could have organized the data to achieve similar results?

309. Can more resources be added?

310. How do you manage time?

311. What is missing?

2.13 Milestone List: Microsoft Office Visio

312. Own known vulnerabilities?

313. Marketing - reach, distribution, awareness?

314. Continuity, supply chain robustness?

315. What specific improvements did you make to the Microsoft Office Visio project proposal since the previous time?

316. How will the milestone be verified?

317. How will you get the word out to customers?

318. How soon can the activity start?

319. Usps (unique selling points)?

320. Milestone pages should display the UserID of the person who added the milestone. Does a report or query exist that provides this audit information?

321. What background experience, skills, and strengths does the team bring to your organization?

322. Describe your organizations strengths and core competencies. What factors will make your organization succeed?

323. Sustaining internal capabilities?

324. Describe the concept of the technology, product or service that will be or has been developed. How will it be used?

325. Gaps in capabilities?

326. Global influences?

327. What has been done so far?

328. Identify critical paths (one or more) and which activities are on the critical path?

329. How late can the activity finish?

330. When will the Microsoft Office Visio project be complete?

2.14 Network Diagram: Microsoft Office Visio

331. Are the gantt chart and/or network diagram updated periodically and used to assess the overall Microsoft Office Visio project timetable?

332. What are the Major Administrative Issues?

333. Review the logical flow of the network diagram. Take a look at which activities you have first and then sequence the activities. Do they make sense?

334. What are the tools?

335. If the Microsoft Office Visio project network diagram cannot change and you have extra personnel resources, what is the BEST thing to do?

336. Where do you schedule uncertainty time?

337. What activities must occur simultaneously with this activity?

338. Will crashing x weeks return more in benefits than it costs?

339. Planning: who, how long, what to do?

340. What is the completion time?

341. Exercise: what is the probability that the Microsoft Office Visio project duration will exceed xx

weeks?

342. What job or jobs could run concurrently?

343. What is the lowest cost to complete this Microsoft Office Visio project in xx weeks?

344. What are the Key Success Factors?

345. What to do and When?

346. What job or jobs precede it?

347. Where do schedules come from?

348. If x is long, what would be the completion time if you break x into two parallel parts of y weeks and z weeks?

2.15 Activity Resource Requirements: Microsoft Office Visio

349. What is the Work Plan Standard?

350. Are there unresolved issues that need to be addressed?

351. Which logical relationship does the PDM use most often?

352. Why do you do that?

353. When does monitoring begin?

354. How many signatures do you require on a check and does this match what is in your policy and procedures?

355. How do you handle petty cash?

356. Time for overtime?

357. Do you use tools like decomposition and rolling-wave planning to produce the activity list and other outputs?

358. What are constraints that you might find during the Human Resource Planning process?

359. Anything else?

360. Other support in specific areas?

361. Organizational Applicability?

2.16 Resource Breakdown Structure: Microsoft Office Visio

362. The list could probably go on, but, the thing that you would most like to know is, How long & How much?

363. Why do you do it?

364. What is Microsoft Office Visio project communication management?

365. What is the primary purpose of the human resource plan?

366. How can this help you with team building?

367. How difficult will it be to do specific activities on this Microsoft Office Visio project?

368. Who will use the system?

369. What is each stakeholders desired outcome for the Microsoft Office Visio project?

370. What are the requirements for resource data?

371. Why is this important?

372. Is predictive resource analysis being done?

373. Who delivers the information?

374. Who is allowed to perform which functions?

375. What can you do to improve productivity?

376. How should the information be delivered?

377. When do they need the information?

378. Why time management?

379. Who is allowed to see what data about which resources?

2.17 Activity Duration Estimates: Microsoft Office Visio

380. What are the nine areas of expertise?

381. Who will provide inputs for it?

382. Would you rate yourself as being risk-averse, risk-neutral, or risk-seeking?

383. Consider the changes in the job market for information technology workers. How does the job market and current state of the economy affect human resource management?

384. Describe a Microsoft Office Visio project that suffered from scope creep. Could it have been avoided?

385. Does a process exist to identify which qualified resources may be attainable?

386. Describe Microsoft Office Visio project integration management in your own words. How does Microsoft Office Visio project integration management relate to the Microsoft Office Visio project life cycle, stakeholders, and the other Microsoft Office Visio project management knowledge areas?

387. Are costs that may be needed to account for Microsoft Office Visio project risks determined?

388. What is pmp certification, and why do you think the number of people earning it has grown so much in the past ten years?

389. Write a oneto two-page paper describing your dream team for this Microsoft Office Visio project. What type of people would you want on your team?

390. Research recruiting and retention strategies at three different companies. What distinguishes one organization from another in this area?

391. What are the three main outputs of quality control?

392. Are Microsoft Office Visio project activities decomposed into manageable components to ensure expected management control?

393. Account for the four frames of organizations. How can they help Microsoft Office Visio project managers understand your organizational context for Microsoft Office Visio projects?

394. What do you think the real problem was in this case?

395. Is the Microsoft Office Visio project performing better or worse than planned?

396. How is the Microsoft Office Visio project doing?

397. What type of activity sequencing method is required for corresponding activities?

398. What is the duration of a milestone?

2.18 Duration Estimating Worksheet: Microsoft Office Visio

399. What utility impacts are there?

400. What is your role?

401. What is an Average Microsoft Office Visio project?

402. Science = process: remember the scientific method?

403. Value pocket identification & quantification what are value pockets?

404. Define the work as completely as possible. What work will be included in the Microsoft Office Visio project?

405. Small or large Microsoft Office Visio project?

406. What work will be included in the Microsoft Office Visio project?

407. Is a construction detail attached (to aid in explanation)?

408. What is cost and Microsoft Office Visio project cost management?

409. What is next?

410. What questions do you have?

411. Do any colleagues have experience with your organization and/or RFPs?

412. Will the Microsoft Office Visio project collaborate with the local community and leverage resources?

413. How should ongoing costs be monitored to try to keep the Microsoft Office Visio project within budget?

2.19 Project Schedule: Microsoft Office Visio

414. What is the difference?

415. Master Microsoft Office Visio project schedule?

416. What is risk?

417. Are key risk mitigation strategies added to the Microsoft Office Visio project schedule?

418. Month Microsoft Office Visio project take?

419. Understand the constraints used in preparing the schedule. Are activities connected because logic dictates the order in which others occur?

420. How do you know that youhave done this right?

421. How can slack be negative?

422. Your Microsoft Office Visio project management plan results in a Microsoft Office Visio project schedule that is too long. If the Microsoft Office Visio project network diagram cannot change and you have extra personnel resources, what is the BEST thing to do?

423. Are you working on the right risks?

424. Are quality inspections and review activities listed in the Microsoft Office Visio project schedule(s)?

425. Is the structure for tracking the Microsoft Office Visio project schedule well defined and assigned to a specific individual?

426. How effectively were issues able to be resolved without impacting the Microsoft Office Visio project Schedule or Budget?

427. Why do you need schedules?

428. What are you counting on?

429. What is the most mis-scheduled part of process?

430. Change management required?

431. Activity charts and bar charts are graphical representations of a Microsoft Office Visio project schedule ...how do they differ?

432. Verify that the update is accurate. Are all remaining durations correct?

2.20 Cost Management Plan: Microsoft Office Visio

433. Are actuals compared against estimates to analyze and correct variances?

434. What is Microsoft Office Visio project management?

435. Does the Microsoft Office Visio project have a Statement of Work?

436. What would you do differently what did not work?

437. Are written status reports provided on a designated frequent basis?

438. Estimating responsibilities – how will the responsibilities for cost estimating be allocated?

439. Are the Microsoft Office Visio project plans updated on a frequent basis?

440. Is Microsoft Office Visio project work proceeding in accordance with the original Microsoft Office Visio project schedule?

441. Best practices implementation – How will change management be applied to this Microsoft Office Visio project?

442. Do Microsoft Office Visio project managers

participating in the Microsoft Office Visio project know the Microsoft Office Visio projects true status first hand?

443. Planning and scheduling responsibilities – How will the responsibilities for planning and scheduling be allocated?

444. Will the forecasts be based on trend analysis and earned value statistics?

445. Are assumptions being identified, recorded, analyzed, qualified and closed?

446. Are meeting minutes captured and sent out after the meeting?

447. Have activity relationships and interdependencies within tasks been adequately identified?

448. Are quality inspections and review activities listed in the Microsoft Office Visio project schedule(s)?

449. What is your organizations history in doing similar tasks?

2.21 Activity Cost Estimates: Microsoft Office Visio

450. How and when do you enter into Microsoft Office Visio project Procurement Management?

451. Where can you get activity reports?

452. How difficult will it be to do specific tasks on the Microsoft Office Visio project?

453. What is the activity inventory?

454. Does the estimator have experience?

455. How do you fund change orders?

456. The impact and what actions were taken?

457. Measurable - are the targets measurable?

458. What are the audit requirements?

459. What were things that you did very well and want to do the same again on the next Microsoft Office Visio project?

460. What areas were overlooked on this Microsoft Office Visio project?

461. Who & what determines the need for contracted services?

462. Are cost subtotals needed?

463. Who determines when the contractor is paid?

464. What makes a good expected result statement?

465. How do you treat administrative costs in the activity inventory?

466. What do you want to know about the stay to know if costs were inappropriately high or low?

467. How do you change activities?

468. Would you hire them again?

2.22 Cost Estimating Worksheet: Microsoft Office Visio

469. What can be included?

470. Does the Microsoft Office Visio project provide innovative ways for stakeholders to overcome obstacles or deliver better outcomes?

471. What costs are to be estimated?

472. How will the results be shared and to whom?

473. Who is best positioned to know and assist in identifying corresponding factors?

474. Is it feasible to establish a control group arrangement?

475. What additional Microsoft Office Visio project(s) could be initiated as a result of this Microsoft Office Visio project?

476. Ask: are others positioned to know, are others credible, and will others cooperate?

477. Identify the timeframe necessary to monitor progress and collect data to determine how the selected measure has changed?

478. What is the purpose of estimating?

479. What happens to any remaining funds not used?

480. What will others want?

481. What is the estimated labor cost today based upon this information?

482. Can a trend be established from historical performance data on the selected measure and are the criteria for using trend analysis or forecasting methods met?

483. Is the Microsoft Office Visio project responsive to community need?

484. Will the Microsoft Office Visio project collaborate with the local community and leverage resources?

485. What info is needed?

2.23 Cost Baseline: Microsoft Office Visio

486. Are there contingencies or conditions related to the acceptance?

487. What is the consequence?

488. Should a more thorough impact analysis be conducted?

489. If you sold 10x widgets on a day, what would the affect on profits be?

490. What threats might prevent you from getting there?

491. Has training and knowledge transfer of the operations organization been completed?

492. Does a process exist for establishing a cost baseline to measure Microsoft Office Visio project performance?

493. How accurate do cost estimates need to be?

494. Has the Microsoft Office Visio project (or Microsoft Office Visio project phase) been evaluated against each objective established in the product description and Integrated Microsoft Office Visio project Plan?

495. Who will use corresponding metrics ?

496. Has the Microsoft Office Visio project documentation been archived or otherwise disposed as described in the Microsoft Office Visio project communication plan?

497. What deliverables come first?

498. Have all approved changes to the Microsoft Office Visio project requirement been identified and impact on the performance, cost, and schedule baselines documented?

499. Review your risk triggers -have your risks changed?

500. Does it impact schedule, cost, quality?

501. What is cost and Microsoft Office Visio project cost management?

2.24 Quality Management Plan: Microsoft Office Visio

502. Is it necessary?

503. What are your organizations current levels and trends for the already stated measures related to financial and marketplace performance?

504. Is this process still needed?

505. Have all necessary approvals been obtained?

506. How is staff trained on the recording of field notes?

507. List your organizations customer contact standards that employees are expected to maintain. How are corresponding standards measured?

508. How does your organization determine the requirements and product/service features important to customers?

509. How does training support what is important to your organization and the individual?

510. What are the established criteria that sampling / testing data are compared against?

511. What are your results for key measures/indicators of accomplishment of organizational strategy?

512. Who gets results of work?

513. What key performance indicators does your organization use to measure, manage, and improve key processes?

514. Are there ways to reduce the time it takes to get something approved?

515. Contradictory information between different documents?

516. Account for the procedures used to verify the data quality of the data being reviewed?

517. Were there any deficiencies / issues identified in the prior years self-assessment?

518. Can the requirements be traced to the appropriate components of the solution, as well as test scripts?

519. Do the data quality objectives communicate the intended program need?

520. Are qmps good forever?

2.25 Quality Metrics: Microsoft Office Visio

521. Is there a set of procedures to capture, analyze and act on quality metrics?

522. How do you communicate results and findings to upper management?

523. How is it being measured?

524. What is the benchmark?

525. How do you measure?

526. Are applicable standards referenced and available?

527. Where is quality now?

528. What is the timeline to meet your goal?

529. Are documents on hand to provide explanations of privacy and confidentiality?

530. How effective are your security tests?

531. Who notifies stakeholders of normal and abnormal results?

532. If the defect rate during testing is substantially higher than that of the previous release (or a similar product), then ask: Did you plan for and actually

improve testing effectiveness?

533. Is quality culture a competitive advantage?

534. How exactly do you define when differences exist?

535. Can visual measures help you to filter visualizations of interest?

536. Have alternatives been defined in the event that failure occurs?

537. Subjective quality component: customer satisfaction, how do you measure it?

538. How should customers provide input?

539. Has trace of defects been initiated?

2.26 Process Improvement Plan: Microsoft Office Visio

540. What is the return on investment?

541. Are you making progress on the improvement framework?

542. To elicit goal statements, do you ask a question such as, What do you want to achieve?

543. What personnel are the champions for the initiative?

544. Does your process ensure quality?

545. Who should prepare the process improvement action plan?

546. If a process improvement framework is being used, which elements will help the problems and goals listed?

547. What lessons have you learned so far?

548. Everyone agrees on what process improvement is, right?

549. What is the test-cycle concept?

550. Are you following the quality standards?

551. What personnel are the sponsors for that

initiative?

552. Where do you want to be?

553. Why quality management?

554. Where are you now?

555. Are you making progress on the goals?

556. Has the time line required to move measurement results from the points of collection to databases or users been established?

557. What is quality and how will you ensure it?

558. Are you meeting the quality standards?

2.27 Responsibility Assignment Matrix: Microsoft Office Visio

559. Most people let you know when others re too busy, and are others really too busy?

560. The already stated responsible for the establishment of budgets and assignment of resources for overhead performance?

561. Microsoft Office Visio projected economic escalation?

562. Changes in the direct base to which overhead costs are allocated?

563. Can the contractor substantiate work package and planning package budgets?

564. Is data disseminated to the contractors management timely, accurate, and usable?

565. Are data elements reconcilable between internal summary reports and reports forwarded to stakeholders?

566. Are records maintained to show how management reserves are used?

567. What are the deliverables?

568. Identify potential or actual overruns and underruns?

569. What are the known stakeholder requirements?

570. Evaluate the performance of operating organizations?

571. Do you need to convince people that its well worth the time and effort?

572. Is budgeted cost for work performed calculated in a manner consistent with the way work is planned?

573. With too many people labeled as doing the work, are there too many hands involved?

2.28 Roles and Responsibilities: Microsoft Office Visio

574. Where are you most strong as a supervisor?

575. What are your major roles and responsibilities in the area of performance measurement and assessment?

576. Are your budgets supportive of a culture of quality data?

577. What areas would you highlight for changes or improvements?

578. Implementation of actions: Who are the responsible units?

579. Do you take the time to clearly define roles and responsibilities on Microsoft Office Visio project tasks?

580. What expectations were met?

581. What is working well within your organizations performance management system?

582. Are Microsoft Office Visio project team roles and responsibilities identified and documented?

583. Was the expectation clearly communicated?

584. Accountabilities: what are the roles and responsibilities of individual team members?

585. Concern: where are you limited or have no authority, where you can not influence?

586. Who is involved?

587. What should you do now to ensure that you are exceeding expectations and excelling in your current position?

588. Influence: what areas of organizational decision making are you able to influence when you do not have authority to make the final decision?

589. Are governance roles and responsibilities documented?

590. What areas of supervision are challenging for you?

591. Attainable / achievable: the goal is attainable; can you actually accomplish the goal?

592. Is there a training program in place for stakeholders covering expectations, roles and responsibilities and any addition knowledge others need to be good stakeholders?

2.29 Human Resource Management Plan: Microsoft Office Visio

593. Have Microsoft Office Visio project team accountabilities & responsibilities been clearly defined?

594. Is it standard practice to formally commit stakeholders to the Microsoft Office Visio project via agreements?

595. Are trade-offs between accepting the risk and mitigating the risk identified?

596. Are cause and effect determined for risks when others occur?

597. Did the Microsoft Office Visio project team have the right skills?

598. Were Microsoft Office Visio project team members involved in detailed estimating and scheduling?

599. Have process improvement efforts been completed before requirements efforts begin?

600. Has a provision been made to reassess Microsoft Office Visio project risks at various Microsoft Office Visio project stages?

601. Quality of people required to meet the forecast needs of the department?

602. Are quality metrics defined?

603. Is an industry recognized support tool(s) being used for Microsoft Office Visio project scheduling & tracking?

604. Are risk triggers captured?

605. How do you determine what key skills and talents are needed to meet the objectives. Is your organization primarily focused on a specific industry?

606. Are issues raised, assessed, actioned, and resolved in a timely and efficient manner?

607. Is the communication plan being followed?

608. Account for the purpose of this Microsoft Office Visio project by describing, at a high-level, what will be done. What is this Microsoft Office Visio project aiming to achieve?

609. How will the Microsoft Office Visio project manage expectations & meet needs and requirements?

610. Are Microsoft Office Visio project team members involved in detailed estimating and scheduling?

611. Were escalated issues resolved promptly?

2.30 Communications Management Plan: Microsoft Office Visio

612. Which stakeholders are thought leaders, influences, or early adopters?

613. What is the stakeholders level of authority?

614. What to learn?

615. Are stakeholders internal or external?

616. Who have you worked with in past, similar initiatives?

617. Timing: when do the effects of the communication take place?

618. Who is involved as you identify stakeholders?

619. How will the person responsible for executing the communication item be notified?

620. What to know?

621. Which team member will work with each stakeholder?

622. Are there common objectives between the team and the stakeholder?

623. How were corresponding initiatives successful?

624. Do you feel a register helps?

625. Do you then often overlook a key stakeholder or stakeholder group?

626. Are others part of the communications management plan?

627. Is there an important stakeholder who is actively opposed and will not receive messages?

628. Conflict resolution -which method when?

629. What steps can you take for a positive relationship?

630. What does the stakeholder need from the team?

631. Who is responsible?

2.31 Risk Management Plan: Microsoft Office Visio

632. Are status updates being made on schedule and are the updates clearly described?

633. Are the participants able to keep up with the workload?

634. How is implementation of risk actions performed?

635. How quickly does this item need to be resolved?

636. Risk probability and impact: how will the probabilities and impacts of risk items be assessed?

637. Which risks should get the attention?

638. What are the chances the event will occur?

639. Who has experience with this?

640. Are the software tools integrated with each other?

641. Degree of confidence in estimated size estimate?

642. Premium on reliability of product?

643. Is the technology to be built new to your organization?

644. What are it-specific requirements?

645. Are the metrics meaningful and useful?

646. Are enough people available?

647. What other risks are created by choosing an avoidance strategy?

648. How is risk monitoring performed?

649. What did not work so well?

2.32 Risk Register: Microsoft Office Visio

650. What can be done about it?

651. What are your key risks/show istoppers and what is being done to manage them?

652. How are risks graded?

653. Risk categories: what are the main categories of risks that should be addressed on this Microsoft Office Visio project?

654. What risks might negatively or positively affect achieving the Microsoft Office Visio project objectives?

655. How well are risks controlled?

656. User involvement: do you have the right users?

657. Having taken action, how did the responses effect change, and where is the Microsoft Office Visio project now?

658. People risk -are people with appropriate skills available to help complete the Microsoft Office Visio project?

659. Does the evidence highlight any areas to advance opportunities or foster good relations. If yes what steps will be taken?

660. What would the impact to the Microsoft Office Visio project objectives be should the risk arise?

661. Recovery actions - planned actions taken once a risk has occurred to allow you to move on. What should you do after?

662. Who is accountable?

663. Are implemented controls working as others should?

664. Are corrective measures implemented as planned?

665. How could corresponding Risk affect the Microsoft Office Visio project in terms of cost and schedule?

666. Preventative actions - planned actions to reduce the likelihood a risk will occur and/or reduce the seriousness should it occur. What should you do now?

667. Market risk -will the new service or product be useful to your organization or marketable to others?

668. Assume the event happens, what is the Most Likely impact?

2.33 Probability and Impact Assessment: Microsoft Office Visio

669. Who should be notified of the occurrence of each of the risk indicators?

670. Is the Microsoft Office Visio project cutting across the entire organization?

671. Has the need for the Microsoft Office Visio project been properly established?

672. How much risk do others need to take?

673. Do you have a mechanism for managing change?

674. What is the probability of the risk occurring?

675. What will be the likely political situation during the life of the Microsoft Office Visio project?

676. Risk urgency assessment -which of your risks could occur soon, or require a longer planning time?

677. Sensitivity analysis -which risks will have the most impact on the Microsoft Office Visio project?

678. What is the level of experience available with your organization?

679. How completely has the customer been identified?

680. Why has this particular mode of contracting been chosen?

681. What is the risk appetite?

682. Have you ascribed a level of confidence to every critical technical objective?

683. Are Microsoft Office Visio project requirements stable?

684. Have you worked with the customer in the past?

685. Which functions, departments, and activities of your organization are going to be affected?

686. Are requirements fully understood by the software engineering team and customers?

687. Does the customer understand the software process?

688. What should be done with non-critical risks?

2.34 Probability and Impact Matrix: Microsoft Office Visio

689. Are compilers and code generators available and suitable for the product to be built?

690. Risk may be made during which step of risk management?

691. How do you define a risk?

692. Does the Microsoft Office Visio project team have experience with the technology to be implemented?

693. What are the ways you measure and evaluate risks?

694. What is the industrial relations prevailing in this organization?

695. Costs associated with late delivery or a defective product?

696. Has something like this been done before?

697. Is security a central objective?

698. To what extent is the chosen technology maturing?

699. How is the risk management process used in practice?

700. How do you analyze the risks in the different types of Microsoft Office Visio projects?

701. Do you have specific methods that you use for each phase of the process?

702. What are the methods to deal with risks?

703. Lay ground work for future returns?

704. During which risk management process is a determination to transfer a risk made?

705. What is the likelihood?

2.35 Risk Data Sheet: Microsoft Office Visio

706. How can hazards be reduced?

707. What if client refuses?

708. What can you do?

709. Do effective diagnostic tests exist?

710. Has a sensitivity analysis been carried out?

711. What were the Causes that contributed?

712. What actions can be taken to eliminate or remove risk?

713. What are you trying to achieve (Objectives)?

714. How reliable is the data source?

715. What will be the consequences if it happens?

716. Will revised controls lead to tolerable risk levels?

717. Who has a vested interest in how you perform as your organization (our stakeholders)?

718. How do you handle product safely?

719. What do people affected think about the need for, and practicality of preventive measures?

720. If it happens, what are the consequences?

721. Are new hazards created?

722. What are the main opportunities available to you that you should grab while you can?

723. What can happen?

724. During work activities could hazards exist?

2.36 Procurement Management Plan: Microsoft Office Visio

725. Are procurement deliverables arriving on time and to specification?

726. Are Microsoft Office Visio project team roles and responsibilities identified and documented?

727. Has a Microsoft Office Visio project Communications Plan been developed?

728. What are your quality assurance overheads?

729. Staffing Requirements?

730. Does the business case include how the Microsoft Office Visio project aligns with your organizations strategic goals & objectives?

731. Were Microsoft Office Visio project team members involved in the development of activity & task decomposition?

732. Has Microsoft Office Visio project success criteria been defined?

733. Are Microsoft Office Visio project team members committed fulltime?

734. Alignment to strategic goals & objectives?

735. Is there a set of procedures defining the scope,

procedures, and deliverables defining quality control?

736. Is there a procurement management plan in place?

737. Does the resource management plan include a personnel development plan?

738. Are any non-compliance issues that exist communicated to your organization?

739. Have the key elements of a coherent Microsoft Office Visio project management strategy been established?

740. Have all unresolved risks been documented?

741. Are the Microsoft Office Visio project team members located locally to the users/stakeholders?

2.37 Source Selection Criteria: Microsoft Office Visio

742. What risks were identified in the proposals?

743. What are the guiding principles for developing an evaluation report?

744. Does the evaluation of any change include an impact analysis; how will the change affect the scope, time, cost, and quality of the goods or services being provided?

745. What are the most common types of rating systems?

746. What are the limitations on pre-competitive range communications?

747. Are evaluators ready to begin this task?

748. Can you prevent comparison of proposals?

749. How do you consolidate reviews and analysis of evaluators?

750. How important is cost in the source selection decision relative to past performance and technical considerations?

751. Have team members been adequately trained?

752. What will you use to capture evaluation and

subsequent documentation?

753. Can you identify proposed teaming partners and/or subcontractors and consider the nature and extent of proposed involvement in satisfying the Microsoft Office Visio project requirements?

754. What is the effect of the debriefing schedule on potential protests?

755. What instructions should be provided regarding oral presentations?

756. What source selection software is your team using?

757. Who is entitled to a debriefing?

758. How should oral presentations be evaluated?

759. When is it appropriate to issue a Draft Request for Proposal (DRFP)?

760. Are considerations anticipated?

761. What should a DRFP include?

2.38 Stakeholder Management Plan: Microsoft Office Visio

762. Have Microsoft Office Visio project team accountabilities & responsibilities been clearly defined?

763. Is there a formal set of procedures supporting Stakeholder Management?

764. Is there general agreement & acceptance of the current status and progress of the Microsoft Office Visio project?

765. Are cause and effect determined for risks when they occur?

766. Are Microsoft Office Visio project contact logs kept up to date?

767. How will you engage this stakeholder and gain commitment?

768. Are non-critical path items updated and agreed upon with the teams?

769. Have all involved Microsoft Office Visio project stakeholders and work groups committed to the Microsoft Office Visio project?

770. Have key stakeholders been identified?

771. Does the Microsoft Office Visio project have a

formal Microsoft Office Visio project Plan?

772. Has the Microsoft Office Visio project manager been identified?

773. Who might be involved in developing a charter?

774. Has a Microsoft Office Visio project Communications Plan been developed?

775. What specific resources will be required for implementation activities?

776. Are parking lot items captured?

777. Has a Microsoft Office Visio project Communications Plan been developed?

778. Are you meeting your customers expectations consistently?

779. Are decisions captured in a decisions log?

780. Are there standards for code development?

2.39 Change Management Plan: Microsoft Office Visio

781. What new behaviours are required?

782. Who should be involved in developing a change management strategy?

783. What does a resilient organization look like?

784. Has the training provider been established?

785. What prerequisite knowledge or training is required?

786. What processes are in place to manage knowledge about the Microsoft Office Visio project?

787. What are the major changes to processes?

788. Who will do the training?

789. Where will the funds come from?

790. How can you best frame the message so that it addresses the audiences interests?

791. How frequently should you repeat the message?

792. Who is the audience for change management activities?

793. What did the people around you say about it?

794. What new competencies will be required for the roles?

795. What are the needs, priorities and special interests of the audience?

796. Has a training need analysis been carried out?

797. Have the systems been configured and tested?

798. Who will be the change levers?

3.0 Executing Process Group: Microsoft Office Visio

799. How do you enter durations, link tasks, and view critical path information?

800. How is Microsoft Office Visio project performance information created and distributed?

801. Why should Microsoft Office Visio project managers strive to make jobs look easy?

802. What are the main types of goods and services being outsourced?

803. In what way has the program come up with innovative measures for problem-solving?

804. Based on your Microsoft Office Visio project communication management plan, what worked well?

805. What will you do to minimize the impact should a risk event occur?

806. If a risk event occurs, what will you do?

807. What are crucial elements of successful Microsoft Office Visio project plan execution?

808. What are the main parts of the scope statement?

809. What is the critical path for this Microsoft Office

Visio project and how long is it?

810. What is in place for ensuring adequate change control on Microsoft Office Visio projects that involve outside contracts?

811. Is the Microsoft Office Visio project making progress in helping to achieve the set results?

812. If action is called for, what form should it take?

813. What are deliverables of your Microsoft Office Visio project?

814. Have operating capacities been created and/or reinforced in partners?

815. How does Microsoft Office Visio project management relate to other disciplines?

816. It under budget or over budget?

817. How do you measure difficulty?

3.1 Team Member Status Report: Microsoft Office Visio

818. Are your organizations Microsoft Office Visio projects more successful over time?

819. How it is to be done?

820. Are the products of your organizations Microsoft Office Visio projects meeting customers objectives?

821. Will the staff do training or is that done by a third party?

822. What specific interest groups do you have in place?

823. Does every department have to have a Microsoft Office Visio project Manager on staff?

824. The problem with Reward & Recognition Programs is that the truly deserving people all too often get left out. How can you make it practical?

825. When a teams productivity and success depend on collaboration and the efficient flow of information, what generally fails them?

826. What is to be done?

827. How can you make it practical?

828. How does this product, good, or service meet the

needs of the Microsoft Office Visio project and your organization as a whole?

829. Are the attitudes of staff regarding Microsoft Office Visio project work improving?

830. Does the product, good, or service already exist within your organization?

831. Is there evidence that staff is taking a more professional approach toward management of your organizations Microsoft Office Visio projects?

832. Why is it to be done?

833. How will resource planning be done?

834. Does your organization have the means (staff, money, contract, etc.) to produce or to acquire the product, good, or service?

835. How much risk is involved?

836. Do you have an Enterprise Microsoft Office Visio project Management Office (EPMO)?

3.2 Change Request: Microsoft Office Visio

837. Which requirements attributes affect the risk to reliability the most?

838. Will new change requests be acknowledged in a timely manner?

839. Should staff call into the helpdesk or go to the website?

840. Screen shots or attachments included in a Change Request?

841. What needs to be communicated?

842. Can static requirements change attributes like the size of the change be used to predict reliability in execution?

843. Are there requirements attributes that are strongly related to the complexity and size?

844. What are the duties of the change control team?

845. Are you implementing itil processes?

846. Who will perform the change?

847. Who is included in the change control team?

848. Where do changes come from?

849. Who can suggest changes?

850. Why do you want to have a change control system?

851. Can you answer what happened, who did it, when did it happen, and what else will be affected?

852. How to get changes (code) out in a timely manner?

853. Will all change requests be unconditionally tracked through this process?

854. Are change requests logged and managed?

855. For which areas does this operating procedure apply?

3.3 Change Log: Microsoft Office Visio

856. Is the requested change request a result of changes in other Microsoft Office Visio project(s)?

857. Do the described changes impact on the integrity or security of the system?

858. How does this change affect scope?

859. When was the request submitted?

860. Is the change request open, closed or pending?

861. When was the request approved?

862. Does the suggested change request represent a desired enhancement to the products functionality?

863. Is the change backward compatible without limitations?

864. Is the change request within Microsoft Office Visio project scope?

865. Is the submitted change a new change or a modification of a previously approved change?

866. Does the suggested change request seem to represent a necessary enhancement to the product?

867. Will the Microsoft Office Visio project fail if the change request is not executed?

868. How does this relate to the standards developed for specific business processes?

869. How does this change affect the timeline of the schedule?

870. Is this a mandatory replacement?

871. Who initiated the change request?

3.4 Decision Log: Microsoft Office Visio

872. What is the line where eDiscovery ends and document review begins?

873. How consolidated and comprehensive a story can you tell by capturing currently available incident data in a central location and through a log of key decisions during an incident?

874. Who will be given a copy of this document and where will it be kept?

875. How do you define success?

876. What makes you different or better than others companies selling the same thing?

877. What eDiscovery problem or issue did your organization set out to fix or make better?

878. It becomes critical to track and periodically revisit both operational effectiveness; Are you noticing all that you need to, and are you interpreting what you see effectively?

879. Does anything need to be adjusted?

880. How does provision of information, both in terms of content and presentation, influence acceptance of alternative strategies?

881. With whom was the decision shared or considered?

882. How does the use a Decision Support System influence the strategies/tactics or costs?

883. What are the cost implications?

884. Do strategies and tactics aimed at less than full control reduce the costs of management or simply shift the cost burden?

885. Behaviors; what are guidelines that the team has identified that will assist them with getting the most out of team meetings?

886. How effective is maintaining the log at facilitating organizational learning?

887. What is your overall strategy for quality control / quality assurance procedures?

888. At what point in time does loss become unacceptable?

889. Meeting purpose; why does this team meet?

890. What was the rationale for the decision?

891. Who is the decisionmaker?

3.5 Quality Audit: Microsoft Office Visio

892. Is there a written procedure for receiving materials?

893. For each device to be reconditioned, are device specifications, such as appropriate engineering drawings, component specifications and software specifications, maintained?

894. Have personnel cleanliness and health requirements been established?

895. Is refuse and garbage adequately stored and disposed of with sufficient frequency to prevent contamination?

896. How does your organization know that the support for its staff is appropriately effective and constructive?

897. What are your supplier audits?

898. What mechanisms exist for identification of staff development needs?

899. How does your organization know that its staff support services planning and management systems are appropriately effective and constructive?

900. What is your organizations greatest strength?

901. How does your organization know that it is appropriately effective and constructive in preparing its staff for organizational aspirations?

902. How does your organization know that its teaching activities (and staff learning) are effectively and constructively enhanced by its activities?

903. How does your organization know that its system for recruiting the best staff possible are appropriately effective and constructive?

904. What are you trying to do?

905. How does your organization know that its systems for meeting staff extracurricular learning support requirements are appropriately effective and constructive?

906. How does your organization know that its system for ensuring that its training activities are appropriately resourced and support is appropriately effective and constructive?

907. Are all employees including salespersons made aware that they must report all complaints received from any source for inclusion in the complaint handling system?

908. What data about organizational performance is routinely collected and reported?

909. Are the policies and processes, as set out in the Quality Audit Manual, properly applied?

910. How does your organization know that its

research planning and management systems are appropriately effective and constructive in enabling quality research outcomes?

911. How does your organization know that its staff entrance standards are appropriately effective and constructive and being implemented consistently?

3.6 Team Directory: Microsoft Office Visio

912. How will the team handle changes?

913. How do unidentified risks impact the outcome of the Microsoft Office Visio project?

914. Timing: when do the effects of communication take place?

915. Have you decided when to celebrate the Microsoft Office Visio projects completion date?

916. How will you accomplish and manage the objectives?

917. Process decisions: do invoice amounts match accepted work in place?

918. Process decisions: which organizational elements and which individuals will be assigned management functions?

919. When will you produce deliverables?

920. Process decisions: are contractors adequately prosecuting the work?

921. Is construction on schedule?

922. Process decisions: are there any statutory or regulatory issues relevant to the timely execution of

work?

923. How does the team resolve conflicts and ensure tasks are completed?

924. Who is the Sponsor?

925. How and in what format should information be presented?

926. Decisions: what could be done better to improve the quality of the constructed product?

927. Do purchase specifications and configurations match requirements?

928. Who are the Team Members?

929. Who should receive information (all stakeholders)?

930. Who will write the meeting minutes and distribute?

931. Why is the work necessary?

3.7 Team Operating Agreement: Microsoft Office Visio

932. What is a Virtual Team?

933. How does teaming fit in with overall organizational goals and meet organizational needs?

934. How will group handle unplanned absences?

935. Why does your organization want to participate in teaming?

936. Do team members reside in more than two countries?

937. Do you post any action items, due dates, and responsibilities on the team website?

938. Do you leverage technology engagement tools group chat, polls, screen sharing, etc.?

939. Do you use a parking lot for any items that are important and outside of the agenda?

940. What are the safety issues/risks that need to be addressed and/or that the team needs to consider?

941. Resource allocation: how will individual team members account for time and expenses, and how will this be allocated in the team budget?

942. Is compensation based on team and individual

performance?

943. Did you draft the meeting agenda?

944. What is the anticipated procedure (recruitment, solicitation of volunteers, or assignment) for selecting team members?

945. Did you delegate tasks such as taking meeting minutes, presenting a topic and soliciting input?

946. Did you prepare participants for the next meeting?

947. Have you set the goals and objectives of the team?

948. Seconds for members to respond?

949. Methodologies: how will key team processes be implemented, such as training, research, work deliverable production, review and approval processes, knowledge management, and meeting procedures?

950. Are there more than two native languages represented by your team?

951. Are there the right people on your team?

3.8 Team Performance Assessment: Microsoft Office Visio

952. To what degree are the relative importance and priority of the goals clear to all team members?

953. To what degree are the teams goals and objectives clear, simple, and measurable?

954. To what degree are staff involved as partners in the improvement process?

955. Effects of crew composition on crew performance: Does the whole equal the sum of its parts?

956. If you are worried about method variance before you collect data, what sort of design elements might you include to reduce or eliminate the threat of method variance?

957. How do you keep key people outside the group informed about its accomplishments?

958. If you have criticized someones work for method variance in your role as reviewer, what was the circumstance?

959. To what degree do team members feel that the purpose of the team is important, if not exciting?

960. How hard do you try to make a good selection?

961. How do you recognize and praise members for contributions?

962. To what degree will new and supplemental skills be introduced as the need is recognized?

963. What are teams?

964. To what degree is the team cognizant of small wins to be celebrated along the way?

965. To what degree do team members frequently explore the teams purpose and its implications?

966. To what degree will team members, individually and collectively, commit time to help themselves and others learn and develop skills?

967. Delaying market entry: how long is too long?

968. Can familiarity breed backup?

969. To what degree do all members feel responsible for all agreed-upon measures?

970. To what degree are corresponding categories of skills either actually or potentially represented across the membership?

971. Do you give group members authority to make at least some important decisions?

3.9 Team Member Performance Assessment: Microsoft Office Visio

972. To what degree does the teams purpose contain themes that are particularly meaningful and memorable?

973. What is the Business Management Oversight Process?

974. What happens if a team member receives a Rating of Unsatisfactory?

975. What is a general description of the processes under performance measurement and assessment?

976. Does the rater (supervisor) have to wait for the interim or final performance assessment review to tell an employee that the employees performance is unsatisfactory?

977. What is a significant fact or event?

978. How effective is training that is delivered through technology-based platforms?

979. Does statute or regulation require the job responsibility?

980. What does collaboration look like?

981. What, if any, steps are available for employees who feel they have been unfairly or inaccurately

rated?

982. To what degree do members articulate the goals beyond the team membership?

983. To what extent are systems and applications (e.g., game engine, mobile device platform) utilized?

984. Why were corresponding selected?

985. Is it clear how goals will be accomplished?

986. Are assessment validation activities performed?

987. To what degree do team members articulate the teams work approach?

988. To what degree are the skill areas critical to team performance present?

989. Are any validation activities performed?

990. How was the determination made for which training platforms would be used (i.e., media selection)?

3.10 Issue Log: Microsoft Office Visio

991. What effort will a change need?

992. Do you feel more overwhelmed by stakeholders?

993. Who reported the issue?

994. Where do team members get information?

995. How often do you engage with stakeholders?

996. What is a change?

997. Do you have members of your team responsible for certain stakeholders?

998. What would have to change?

999. What is the status of the issue?

1000. How were past initiatives successful?

1001. Is access to the Issue Log controlled?

1002. Who are the members of the governing body?

1003. How is this initiative related to other portfolios, programs, or Microsoft Office Visio projects?

1004. Persistence; will users learn a work around or will they be bothered every time?

1005. Why do you manage human resources?

1006. Can you think of other people who might have concerns or interests?

1007. Who is the stakeholder?

4.0 Monitoring and Controlling Process Group: Microsoft Office Visio

1008. Did it work?

1009. What were things that you did very well and want to do the same again on the next Microsoft Office Visio project?

1010. How will staff learn how to use the deliverables?

1011. What areas does the group agree are the biggest success on the Microsoft Office Visio project?

1012. Do the partners have sufficient financial capacity to keep up the benefits produced by the programme?

1013. How are you doing?

1014. Do clients benefit (change) from the services?

1015. How is agile Microsoft Office Visio project management done?

1016. Feasibility: how much money, time, and effort can you put into this?

1017. Purpose: toward what end is the evaluation being conducted?

1018. Where is the Risk in the Microsoft Office Visio project?

1019. Are there areas that need improvement?

1020. Are the services being delivered?

1021. How was the program set-up initiated?

1022. Are the necessary foundations in place to ensure the sustainability of the results of the programme?

1023. How is agile portfolio management done?

1024. Key stakeholders to work with. How many potential communications channels exist on the Microsoft Office Visio project?

4.1 Project Performance Report: Microsoft Office Visio

1025. To what degree does the teams work approach provide opportunity for members to engage in open interaction?

1026. To what degree are the goals realistic?

1027. How will procurement be coordinated with other Microsoft Office Visio project aspects, such as scheduling and performance reporting?

1028. To what degree do the relationships of the informal organization motivate taskrelevant behavior and facilitate task completion?

1029. To what degree does the teams work approach provide opportunity for members to engage in fact-based problem solving?

1030. To what degree does the information network communicate information relevant to the task?

1031. How can Microsoft Office Visio project sustainability be maintained?

1032. To what degree does the team possess adequate membership to achieve its ends?

1033. To what degree are the goals ambitious?

1034. To what degree does the task meet individual

needs?

1035. To what degree will the approach capitalize on and enhance the skills of all team members in a manner that takes into consideration other demands on members of the team?

1036. To what degree do team members agree with the goals, relative importance, and the ways in which achievement will be measured?

1037. To what degree can team members meet frequently enough to accomplish the teams ends?

1038. To what degree can team members frequently and easily communicate with one another?

1039. To what degree are fresh input and perspectives systematically caught and added (for example, through information and analysis, new members, and senior sponsors)?

1040. To what degree are the demands of the task compatible with and converge with the mission and functions of the formal organization?

4.2 Variance Analysis: Microsoft Office Visio

1041. Do you identify potential or actual budget-based and time-based schedule variances?

1042. Are all budgets assigned to control accounts?

1043. Are there changes in the direct base to which overhead costs are allocated?

1044. Are there quarterly budgets with quarterly performance comparisons?

1045. Are meaningful indicators identified for use in measuring the status of cost and schedule performance?

1046. What can be the cause of an increase in costs?

1047. Are procedures for variance analysis documented and consistently applied at the control account level and selected WBS and organizational levels at least monthly as a routine task?

1048. How are material, labor, and overhead standards set?

1049. Did an existing competitor change strategy?

1050. Who are responsible for overhead performance control of related costs?

1051. Does the contractors system identify work accomplishment against the schedule plan?

1052. Are the wbs and organizational levels for application of the Microsoft Office Visio projected overhead costs identified?

1053. Are there externalities from having some customers, even if they are unprofitable in the short run?

1054. What does a favorable labor efficiency variance mean?

1055. How do you evaluate the impact of schedule changes, work around, et?

1056. Can process improvements lead to unfavorable variances?

1057. Is cost and schedule performance measurement done in a consistent, systematic manner?

1058. What is the expected future profitability of each customer?

1059. Favorable or unfavorable variance?

4.3 Earned Value Status: Microsoft Office Visio

1060. Validation is a process of ensuring that the developed system will actually achieve the stakeholders desired outcomes; Are you building the right product? What do you validate?

1061. What is the unit of forecast value?

1062. How much is it going to cost by the finish?

1063. When is it going to finish?

1064. Are you hitting your Microsoft Office Visio projects targets?

1065. If earned value management (EVM) is so good in determining the true status of a Microsoft Office Visio project and Microsoft Office Visio project its completion, why is it that hardly any one uses it in information systems related Microsoft Office Visio projects?

1066. Earned value can be used in almost any Microsoft Office Visio project situation and in almost any Microsoft Office Visio project environment. it may be used on large Microsoft Office Visio projects, medium sized Microsoft Office Visio projects, tiny Microsoft Office Visio projects (in cut-down form), complex and simple Microsoft Office Visio projects and in any market sector. some people, of course, know all about earned value, they have used it for years - but perhaps not as effectively as they could have?

1067. How does this compare with other Microsoft Office Visio projects?

1068. Where are your problem areas?

1069. Verification is a process of ensuring that the developed system satisfies the stakeholders agreements and specifications; Are you building the product right? What do you verify?

1070. Where is evidence-based earned value in your organization reported?

4.4 Risk Audit: Microsoft Office Visio

1071. What responsibilities for quality, errors, and outcomes have been delegated to staff (or others) without adequate oversight?

1072. Do staff understand the extent of duty of care?

1073. Is the number of people on the Microsoft Office Visio project team adequate to do the job?

1074. Do you meet all obligations relating to funds secured from grants, loans and sponsors?

1075. Do the people have the right combinations of skills?

1076. Number of users of the product?

1077. What are the differences and similarities between strategic and operational risks in your organization?

1078. To what extent are auditors influenced by the business risk assessment in the audit process, and how can auditors create more effective mental models to more fully examine contradictory evidence?

1079. Have all possible risks/hazards been identified (including injury to staff, damage to equipment, impact on others in the community)?

1080. Are all programs planned and conducted

according to recognized safety standards?

1081. Do you have proper induction processes for all new paid staff and volunteers who have a specific role and responsibility?

1082. Should additional substantive testing be conducted because of the risk audit results?

1083. What are risks and how do you manage them?

1084. Does the customer understand the process?

1085. Are requirements fully understood by the team and customers?

1086. If applicable; does the software interface with new or unproven hardware or unproven vendor products?

1087. Who is responsible for what?

1088. Do you record and file all audits?

1089. For paid staff, does your organization comply with the minimum conditions for employment and/or the applicable modern award?

1090. What risk does not having unique identification present?

4.5 Contractor Status Report: Microsoft Office Visio

1091. How is risk transferred?

1092. Who can list a Microsoft Office Visio project as organization experience, your organization or a previous employee of your organization?

1093. What is the average response time for answering a support call?

1094. Are there contractual transfer concerns?

1095. What was the budget or estimated cost for your organizations services?

1096. If applicable; describe your standard schedule for new software version releases. Are new software version releases included in the standard maintenance plan?

1097. How long have you been using the services?

1098. What was the actual budget or estimated cost for your organizations services?

1099. What process manages the contracts?

1100. What was the overall budget or estimated cost?

1101. What was the final actual cost?

1102. Describe how often regular updates are made to the proposed solution. Are corresponding regular updates included in the standard maintenance plan?

1103. How does the proposed individual meet each requirement?

1104. What are the minimum and optimal bandwidth requirements for the proposed solution?

4.6 Formal Acceptance: Microsoft Office Visio

1105. Was the Microsoft Office Visio project work done on time, within budget, and according to specification?

1106. Was business value realized?

1107. Have all comments been addressed?

1108. Who would use it?

1109. Was the Microsoft Office Visio project goal achieved?

1110. Do you buy pre-configured systems or build your own configuration?

1111. Does it do what client said it would?

1112. Did the Microsoft Office Visio project achieve its MOV?

1113. Does it do what Microsoft Office Visio project team said it would?

1114. Who supplies data?

1115. Is formal acceptance of the Microsoft Office Visio project product documented and distributed?

1116. Was the client satisfied with the Microsoft Office

Visio project results?

1117. What is the Acceptance Management Process?

1118. What can you do better next time?

1119. What was done right?

1120. General estimate of the costs and times to complete the Microsoft Office Visio project?

1121. What lessons were learned about your Microsoft Office Visio project management methodology?

1122. What are the requirements against which to test, Who will execute?

1123. Do you perform formal acceptance or burn-in tests?

1124. What function(s) does it fill or meet?

5.0 Closing Process Group: Microsoft Office Visio

1125. How well did the chosen processes produce the expected results?

1126. What is the Microsoft Office Visio project Management Process?

1127. Is there a clear cause and effect between the activity and the lesson learned?

1128. What were things that you need to improve?

1129. Is this an updated Microsoft Office Visio project Proposal Document?

1130. What is an Encumbrance?

1131. What was learned?

1132. How well defined and documented were the Microsoft Office Visio project management processes you chose to use?

1133. Is this a follow-on to a previous Microsoft Office Visio project?

1134. Are there funding or time constraints?

1135. What were things that you did very well and want to do the same again on the next Microsoft Office Visio project?

1136. What is the amount of funding and what Microsoft Office Visio project phases are funded?

1137. What business situation is being addressed?

1138. Did the Microsoft Office Visio project team have enough people to execute the Microsoft Office Visio project plan?

1139. When will the Microsoft Office Visio project be done?

1140. Just how important is your work to the overall success of the Microsoft Office Visio project?

5.1 Procurement Audit: Microsoft Office Visio

1141. Can changes be made to automatic disbursement programs without proper approval of management?

1142. Was the overall procurement done within a reasonable time?

1143. Did the additional works introduce minor or non-substantial changes to performance, as described in the contract documents?

1144. Are known obligations, such as salaries and contracts, encumbered at the beginning of the year?

1145. When competitive dialogue was used, did the contracting authority provide sufficient justification for the use of this procedure and was the contract actually particularly complex?

1146. Are proper financing arrangements taken?

1147. Is there management monitoring of transactions and balances?

1148. Is the issuance of purchase orders scheduled so that orders are not issued daily?

1149. Were the documents received scrutinised for completion and adherence to stated conditions before the tenders were evaluated?

1150. Are cases of double payment duly prevented and corrected?

1151. Was suitability of candidates accurately assessed?

1152. Do staff involved in the various stages of the process have the appropriate skills and training to perform duties effectively?

1153. Has alternatives been considered for the specified procurement Microsoft Office Visio project?

1154. Are internal control mechanisms performed before payments?

1155. Are there mechanisms in place to evaluate the performance of the departments suppliers?

1156. Audits: when was your last independent public accountant (ipa) audit and what were the results?

1157. Are payment generated from computer programs reviewed by supervisory personnel prior to distribution?

1158. Were standards, certifications and evidence required admissible?

1159. Are sub-criteria clearly indicated?

1160. Was the estimated contract value in line with the final cost of the contract awarded?

5.2 Contract Close-Out: Microsoft Office Visio

1161. Have all contract records been included in the Microsoft Office Visio project archives?

1162. Parties: Authorized?

1163. Change in knowledge?

1164. How does it work?

1165. Change in circumstances?

1166. How is the contracting office notified of the automatic contract close-out?

1167. What is capture management?

1168. Change in attitude or behavior?

1169. Why Outsource?

1170. Has each contract been audited to verify acceptance and delivery?

1171. Was the contract complete without requiring numerous changes and revisions?

1172. Have all contracts been completed?

1173. Was the contract type appropriate?

1174. Have all acceptance criteria been met prior to final payment to contractors?

1175. Are the signers the authorized officials?

1176. What happens to the recipient of services?

1177. How/when used ?

1178. Have all contracts been closed?

1179. Was the contract sufficiently clear so as not to result in numerous disputes and misunderstandings?

1180. Parties: who is involved?

5.3 Project or Phase Close-Out: Microsoft Office Visio

1181. Planned remaining costs?

1182. In addition to assessing whether the Microsoft Office Visio project was successful, it is equally critical to analyze why it was or was not fully successful. Are you including this?

1183. Who are the Microsoft Office Visio project stakeholders and what are roles and involvement?

1184. What is a Risk?

1185. What was expected from each stakeholder?

1186. Was the user/client satisfied with the end product?

1187. What information did each stakeholder need to contribute to the Microsoft Office Visio projects success?

1188. What were the desired outcomes?

1189. Can the lesson learned be replicated?

1190. What security considerations needed to be addressed during the procurement life cycle?

1191. Does the lesson educate others to improve performance?

1192. Were cost budgets met?

1193. What information is each stakeholder group interested in?

1194. Was the schedule met?

1195. Is the lesson significant, valid, and applicable?

1196. Planned completion date?

1197. What advantages do the an individual interview have over a group meeting, and vice-versa?

1198. What can you do better next time, and what specific actions can you take to improve?

1199. Is the lesson based on actual Microsoft Office Visio project experience rather than on independent research?

1200. When and how were information needs best met?

5.4 Lessons Learned: Microsoft Office Visio

1201. How well was Microsoft Office Visio project status communicated throughout your involvement in the Microsoft Office Visio project?

1202. What is below the surface?

1203. What are the internal fiscal constraints?

1204. How clear were you on your role in the Microsoft Office Visio project?

1205. How timely were Progress Reports provided to the Microsoft Office Visio project Manager by Team Members?

1206. Were the Microsoft Office Visio project goals attained?

1207. What is the expected lifespan of the deliverable?

1208. Was the Microsoft Office Visio project significantly delayed/hampered by outside dependencies (outside to the Microsoft Office Visio project, that is)?

1209. What solutions or recommendations can you offer that would have improved some aspect of the Microsoft Office Visio project?

1210. Who managed most of the communication

within the Microsoft Office Visio project?

1211. Are there any data that you have overlooked in identifying lessons?

1212. How well did the scope of the Microsoft Office Visio project match what was defined in the Microsoft Office Visio project Proposal?

1213. What were the main bottlenecks on the process?

1214. What is your organizational ideology?

1215. What were the most significant issues on this Microsoft Office Visio project?

1216. How effectively were issues resolved before escalation was necessary?

1217. How adequately involved did you feel in Microsoft Office Visio project decisions?

1218. How useful was the format and content of the Microsoft Office Visio project Status Report to you?

1219. Were the Microsoft Office Visio project objectives met (if not, briefly account for what wasnt met)?

Index

community	150, 181, 189, 255
companies	1, 179, 232
company	7, 40, 60, 96, 101, 113, 120, 132
compare	70, 76, 115, 117, 254
compared	184, 192
comparing	44
comparison	10, 218
compatible	230, 250
compelling	36
competitor	251
compilers	212
complaint	103, 235
complaints	235
complete	1, 8, 10, 25, 31, 144, 167-168, 171, 173, 208, 260, 265
completed	11, 28, 32, 36-37, 51, 162, 167, 190, 202, 238, 265
completely	60, 102, 180, 210
completion	31, 34, 155, 162, 172-173, 237, 249, 253, 263, 268
complex	7, 125, 145, 253, 263
complexity	40, 164, 228
compliance	41-42, 67, 128, 130, 158
comply	32, 256
component	103-104, 195, 234
components	43, 52, 179, 193
compute	11
computer	157, 264
computing	64, 102
concept	156, 171, 196
concepts	157
concern	78, 106, 201
concerned	22
concerns	16, 117, 128, 246, 257
concise	149
condition	89, 143
conditions	37, 85, 144, 190, 256, 263
conduct	44
conducted	81, 157, 164, 190, 247, 255-256
confidence	206, 211
configure	118
configured	223
confirm	10, 50
Conflict	205
conflicts	151, 238

Microsoft   1-13, 16-38, 40, 42-48, 50-51, 53-57, 59-60, 62-72, 75-84, 86-88, 90-92, 94-97, 100, 102-104, 106-109, 112-113, 115-117, 119-120, 122-125, 127, 130-131, 133-151, 153-157, 159, 161, 164-174, 176, 178-186, 188-192, 194, 196, 198, 200, 202-204, 206, 208-214, 216-222, 224-228, 230, 232, 234, 237, 239, 241, 243, 245, 247-249, 251-255, 257, 259-265, 267-270

migrating   69
migration   99
milestone   3, 147, 170, 179
milestones   27, 139, 147, 168
miners 60
minimize   224
minimizing   122
minimum   256, 258
Mining 58
minutes   33, 83, 185, 238, 240
missed 101
missing 169
mission 57, 60, 103, 137, 250
mitigate   156
mitigating   202
mitigation   119, 144, 182
mobile 244
modeling   16, 115
models 20, 51, 66, 255
moderate   106
modern   256
modified   84
modify 65
moment   101
moments   56
momentum   101
monetary   23
monitor   74, 86-87, 188
monitored   90, 166, 181
monitoring   6, 90, 93, 149, 174, 207, 247, 263
monthly   163, 251
months 80, 83
motivate   98, 112, 249
motivation   22
moving   103
Mozilla 92
multiple   16

Made in the USA
Monee, IL
17 October 2021